Carbon Folly

CO2 emission sources and options

Second Edition

Published by TSAugust

Library of Congress Control Number 2008900543

Dears, Donn D.
Carbon Folly
Includes index
1. Greenhouse Gasses
2. CO2 Emissions
3. Cap & Trade
4. Nuclear Power
5. Coal Fired Power
6. Renewable Energy

ISBN 978-0-9815119-1-7

TSAugust

Second Edition
First Printing

Dedicated to,
Marion the love of my life who is missed beyond belief.

CONTENTS

"Facts are stubborn things; and whatever may be our wishes, our inclinations, or the desires of our passion, they cannot alter the state of facts and evidence."

President John Adams

"It was the great tragedy of science that a beautiful hypothesis can be slain by an ugly fact."

T. H. Huxley

Facts lead to truth.

TSAugust

Foreword

This book does not address global warming per se. Instead, it asks the question:

Is it possible to cut CO_2 emissions 80%? Or by 60%? Or by any significant amount?

There are other Green House Gasses (GHG) besides CO_2, but CO_2 represents the bulk of GHG and is used throughout as a surrogate for all GHG's. (See Appendix A for details of carbon equivalents.)

Information in this book is factually correct. People may try to generate different facts and attempt to reach conclusions different from those drawn here, but an objective analysis will show that the conclusions drawn here are virtually irrefutable.

There is no attempt to denigrate current alternative technologies, such as solar and geothermal. Solar, for example, should be very useful in the Southwest.

There is, however, a need to put these technologies in perspective. These alternative technologies have limitations and the limitations need to be understood before national policies are implemented based on flawed assumptions.

Enacting cap & trade regulations if technologies do not exist to significantly cut CO_2 could be a national disaster.

Once the genie is out of the bottle it will be difficult to put him back. What happens in a few years if Congress determines that CO_2 emissions can't be cut? How do they unravel the actions that have been set in motion?

How, for example, will the market for CO_2 credits or permits be shut down after billions of dollars have been invested in them?

Shouldn't we be certain that technologies exist for cutting CO_2 emissions before establishing cap & trade regulations?

CARBON FOLLY

Introduction

People ask why I wrote *Carbon Folly*. My best reply is to outline the current issues surrounding CO2 emissions and then provide a brief overview of my experiences dealing with the equipment and customers involved with producing and supplying energy.

The reason for writing *Carbon Folly* now is the huge effort underway to have the government control CO2 emissions. It's absurd to think it's possible to cut CO2 emissions 80% when technologies do not exist for accomplishing such a feat.

Many Americans have little understanding of what is involved with attempting to dramatically cut CO2 emissions. Yet, the House has enacted Cap & Trade legislation (Waxman-Markey HR 2454) and the Senate is poised to follow suit.

Additionally, the United Nations has scheduled a meeting to create a new treaty, often referred to as Kyoto II, to require countries to cut CO2 emissions 80% by 2050. This new treaty will result in tremendous pressure on the United States to commit to dramatic cuts in CO2 emissions—even if China and India do not adopt targets for cutting CO2.

President Obama has said, "My presidency will mark a new chapter in America's leadership on climate change … That will start with a federal cap and trade system."

This doesn't bode well for America's future.

Carbon Folly provides Americans with the information they need to make judgments about cap & trade legislation.

1

Introduction

My first job after graduating from college was as a test engineer at General Electric in Schenectady, New York. It was the test engineer's job to test the large steam turbines and generators before they were shipped to utility customers.

Both the turbines and generators were tested at speed, which was usually 3600 rpm.

Special steam lines ran to the turbine test stands. Each turbine had vibration readings taken as it was brought to speed, stopping if the vibration became excessive. These readings were used to calculate the position and size of balance weights. After each run, a test engineer would climb into the turbine casing to insert or readjust a small weight that was inserted into the grooves cut in the wheel holding the buckets. This process was repeated until the turbine ran without noticeable vibration.

The turbine's hydraulic controls were operated to be certain they functioned properly.

Each generator rotor was about fifty feet long, and was mounted in a balance pit where it was brought to speed. As with the turbine, balance weights were inserted in grooves cut at the end of the rotor. Each generator rotor was assembled with the stator and run at speed in a hydrogen atmosphere that reduced wind resistance. It was tested electrically to ensure it performed properly. The insulation was given a high potential test after the test engineer made the electrical connections under the generator.

A test engineering job wasn't glamorous. Much of the work involved dragging cables around the test area, climbing into turbines that were still at around 150° F, and working twelve hour night shifts.

Introduction

Subsequently I worked in manufacturing and sales at the Transformer Division which manufactured distribution and power transformers, voltage regulators, cut outs and lightning arresters for utility customers.

These, together with switchgear and capacitors, are the building blocks of transmission and distribution systems, including the grid.

A few years after my assignment in Schenectady, a generator rotor with an undetected flaw in the forging exploded, sending huge chunks of steel flying several hundred feet. The test engineer was killed, though he was the only casualty.

My assignments in the jet engine, locomotive, DC motor and Naval Ordinance businesses, were not directly relevant to my background in energy issues and have been skipped over here.

Later, as general manager of a business located in the Middle West with a few thousand employees that serviced steam and gas turbines, as well as electrical equipment, I had an opportunity to see firsthand how the equipment was used by customers. Naturally I spent time in steel mills and power plants where some of the service work was done on-site at the steel mill or utility.

Two examples may be of interest.

We had a contract for servicing a large utility substation. Each transformer was tested and oil samples taken to ascertain whether the oil needed to be treated. The work included cleaning the insulators above the substation. Great care was taken to ensure that all electric circuits were cut and that the transformers and switchgear had been grounded.

Introduction

I was at the work site to see the work in progress when one of our workers asked if I wouldn't like to go with him to see how he was cleaning the insulators. I couldn't avoid the challenge so I climbed into the bucket with the operator. He instantly raised the bucket to the fully extended vertical position, high above the substation. He and others had a good laugh at my expense as I gripped the bucket while trying to be nonchalant.

While still in the Middle West, I had an opportunity to go underground at a coal mine. After dressing and receiving safety instructions we took the elevator cage to the bottom of the mine.

I was then led along a tunnel to the mine face. The coal seam was less than five feet high, so it was necessary to walk bent over, sloshing though water and muck for several hundred feet. At the face of the mine the rotating drum of the Heliminer, with teeth mounted on the drum, was cutting chunks of coal from the seam, while also scooping the chunks onto the Heliminer and moving them to the back where the coal was dumped into a shuttle car.

The shuttle car transported the coal back to where it could be moved to the surface on a conveyor belt.

These men have to be admired for the work they do under the conditions in which they work. Returning to the surface I realized how coal dust permeates everything as I washed away the coal from my face and saw coal dust around my socks and ankles that had supposedly been protected by coveralls.

I also had an opportunity to go underground at a salt mine located in Cleveland, Ohio, where the mine stretched out underneath Lake Erie. The contrast with the coal mine was startling. It used the pillar method of mining so there were

4

relatively high ceilings, the mine was clean and the air was easy to breath.

I then had an opportunity to establish service companies in the Middle East, Europe and the Far East.

GE gas turbines were used by the oil industry for pumping and other applications, and by utilities for generating electricity. This equipment needed to be serviced which was an important reason for establishing these service locations.

On one trip to Bahrain a small group of us chartered an airplane so we could obtain a better view of the oil infrastructure and power generating facilities in the eastern province of Saudi Arabia. We flew over Dammam and Dhahran and then over the oil refinery and oil terminals at Ras Tanura.

Flying at a relative low level we had a bumpy ride over the oil refinery because of the updrafts, but it was well worth the turbulence to obtain a close up view of such an important facility.

This was several years before terrorism had become prevalent, but even so, I have always wondered why the Saudi air force allowed us to fly over one of their most important facilities.

At the time, Ras Tanura was Saudi Arabia's largest oil terminal for exporting oil. Since then another terminal has been built at al Jubayl, north of Ras Tanura, while a pipeline has been built from Abqaiq to Yanbu on the Red Sea, where oil is refined and shipped via the Red Sea.

I also visited Aberdeen, Scotland and Rotterdam, the Netherlands to determine whether we should establish facilities

Introduction

at these locations to service equipment from the oil platforms located in the North Sea.

Other opportunities were explored around the Middle East and in major shipping centers such as Singapore.

The purpose of this introduction is to establish that the book *Carbon Folly* is based on considerable personal experience and sound engineering, coupled with extensive research. *Carbon Folly* should also put in perspective all the media hype and hot air from liberal politicians clamoring for dramatic cuts in CO2 emissions.

This book does not address global warming per se. Instead, it asks the question:

Is it possible to cut CO2 emissions 80%?

I believe everything in *Carbon Folly* is factually correct, but if you find an error I hope you will send me an email telling me about what you have found.

People may try to generate different facts and attempt to reach conclusions different from those drawn here, but an objective analysis will show that the conclusions drawn here are virtually irrefutable.

Donn Dears

CARBON FOLLY

PART ONE

Chapter 1

The Controversy

The absurdity of cap & trade legislation or carbon taxes is a testament to the conceit of bureaucrats and liberal politicians.

History is replete with grandiose schemes that proved to be unworkable when the then current technologies couldn't support the ideas in vogue at that time.

Leonardo da Vinci envisioned that man could fly. He produced many drawings to this effect. Though he was right about the possibility of flight, the technology was not then available to allow man to fly.

De Lesseps believed a canal could be built across Panama. Unfortunately the technologies were lacking and his venture ended in failure. It was resurrected when the United States brought new skills and technologies, largely medical, to bear on the problem.

Jules Verne envisioned going to the moon and traveling underwater for great distances, but the technologies were lacking for either idea to become a reality during his lifetime.

Today we are confronted with a dilemma. If global warming is caused by rising atmospheric levels of CO_2, can we cut CO_2 emissions while still providing mankind with the electricity it needs to allow huge numbers of people escape debilitating poverty?

Once again, the answer revolves around available technologies. Unless the technologies exist to cut CO_2 emissions while still allowing increased generation of electricity we are faced with a Hobson's choice. Allow global warming to continue - or - condemn increasing millions to poverty.

Such a choice isn't necessary if either of two conditions are true.

The Controversy

1. If CO2 is not the primary cause of global warming there is no need to cut CO2 emissions, or:

2. If technologies exist that allow cutting CO2 emissions while also increasing the generation of electricity, CO2 emissions can be cut without harming people.

There is a bias in this book that global warming is not being caused primarily by GHG emissions and that we can focus on improving energy efficiency to improve productivity and living conditions, rather than on cutting CO2 emissions. This favors alternative 1 where there is no need to cut CO2 emissions.

(See Exhibit I)

With respect to alternative 2, *Carbon Folly* establishes that technologies <u>do not</u> currently exist to allow large reductions in CO2 emissions while increasing the generation of electricity. Given this to be true, a choice must be made: Allow continued accumulation of CO2 in the atmosphere or condemn millions to poverty.

There are other Green House Gasses (GHG) besides CO2, but CO2 represents the bulk of GHG and is used throughout as a surrogate for all GHG's. (See Appendix A for details of carbon equivalents.)

Carbon Folly concludes that trying to force the cutting of CO2 emissions will harm millions of people worldwide, and be very harmful to the United States.

Some people will respond; "it's better to do something rather than nothing at all."

First, *Carbon Folly* doesn't recommend doing nothing.

What it does recommend is to make improvements in energy efficiency so as to improve the United States' productivity and competitiveness. To the extent improvements in energy efficiency reduce CO2 emissions, so much the better.

8

EXHIBIT I

Some reasons why CO2 may not be the primary cause of Global Warming.

Temperatures around 1100 AD were higher than they are today, while CO2 concentrations in the atmosphere were 278 ppm,[1] that is, at pre- industrial revolution levels.

- Greenland was settled and the settlement flourished, but was then abandoned when temperatures fell during the little Ice Age.

The Little Ice Age saw much lower temperatures until the early 1800's while CO2 concentrations in the atmosphere were 278 ppm (i.e., at pre-industrial revolution levels).

- Remember the picture of George Washington crossing the Delaware? There were large ice flows in the river that are no longer there.
- Remember Hans Brinker or the Silver Skates? A book about ice skating on frozen canals in the Netherlands, a practice that is no longer common as the canals freeze much less frequently.

The world's temperatures have been more or less constant for the past 8 to 10 years, while CO2 levels in the atmosphere have continued to rise.

- If temperatures remain constant while CO2 levels rise, it would suggest there is little linkage between the two.

These are not meant to be solid scientific proof that CO2 emissions are not affecting temperatures, but merely to explain why there is a bias in this book that CO2 is not the primary cause for temperatures having risen during the last century.

The report *Climate Change Reconsidered,* published by the Heartland Institute, provides detailed scientific reasons for concluding that CO2 is not the main cause of climate change.

The Controversy

It also recommends devoting our resources to developing breakthrough technologies.

Second, it's important to analyze what is meant by "doing something."

Does this include wasting resources?

Why take actions that will hurt economic growth when those actions can't affect global warming? All the pronouncements from those favoring action say that the world will suffer a disaster if worldwide CO_2 emissions aren't reduced 50% below 1990 levels.

According to them, CO_2 emissions <u>must</u> be reduced by at least 50% worldwide to prevent a disaster.

Or, stated differently: If CO_2 emissions aren't cut by 50%, the disaster can't be avoided.

If disaster can't be avoided, wouldn't it be better to expend resources doing those things that would mitigate the impact of global warming?

A second response to this book is likely to be: "Isn't this book just more industry sponsored misinformation about why something can't be done?"

Industry has had a track record of saying things couldn't be done only to turn around and do them when government mandated the change. The automobile industry said it couldn't add seat belts, but then added them when they were told to do so. They also said it was impossible to improve gasoline mileage; but they did so.

Industry has often been its own worst enemy by taking negative positions on important issues.

It's against this background that *Carbon Folly* tries to demonstrate how difficult it will be to cut CO_2 emissions by 80% or by any significant amount.

The Controversy

But, rather than being negative, *Carbon Folly* suggests a positive solution to America's need for improved energy efficiency or intensity.

Carbon Folly proposes an alternative to punitive, economy destroying cap & trade regulations and carbon taxes by recognizing the huge potential benefits from new, breakthrough technologies— breakthrough technologies that can alter the world in which we live.

Shouldn't we spend our efforts developing breakthrough technologies for improving carbon intensity and energy efficiency?

Shouldn't our resources be spent on achieving economic growth and reducing poverty?

Shouldn't America focus on research that can produce breakthrough technologies—technologies that can change the world?

A recent advertisement showed a man with Leonardo da Vinci's feathered wings clamped to his body jumping from a bridge in an attempt to fly. He assumed that da Vinci's feathered wings would work. They didn't.

Today, America is poised on the edge of a precipice ready to jump into the abyss while assuming we have the technologies needed to cut CO_2 emissions and simultaneously produce sufficient electricity to meet our growing needs.

Virtually every newspaper and magazine article, as well as the press releases from organizations such as the Pew Charitable Trusts (Pew) and the Natural Resources Defense Council (NRDC), presume it's possible to reduce CO_2 emissions by 80%. But what if it's not possible to reduce emissions by this amount? Or by 60%? Or by 50%? Or by any significant amount?

In proposing cap & trade legislation, have President Obama and Congress considered whether cuts in CO_2 emissions by up to 80% are possible? Or do the president and Congress merely accept the presumptuous utterances of Pew, the NRDC, Al Gore and the UN?

11

The Controversy

It would be like starting to drive to a destination on a dead-end road. We would come to the end of the road long before reaching our destination. Wouldn't that be a waste of resources?

Meanwhile the U.S. Environmental Protection Agency is poised to issue regulations and rules to force the United States to dramatically cut CO_2 emissions. In August 2008 the EPA issued an Advanced Notice of Proposed Rulemaking (ANPR) *"Regulating Greenhouse Gas Emissions under the Clean Air Act"*.

The ANPR went into great detail about how CO_2 emissions should be cut. EPA regulations could extend to schools, large family homes, churches, fork lift trucks and lawnmowers. [2] While not stating precisely how much CO_2 emissions should be cut, it referenced the United Nations CO_2 stabilization program calling for an 80% cut.

In spite of the foregoing, there is one proven technology that could potentially cut CO_2 emissions by 80%.

The proven technology is nuclear energy.

If the United States built 350 new nuclear power plants by 2050, CO_2 emissions could be dramatically cut; perhaps by as much as 80%.

But there is little chance this will happen, as will be explained in Part Two.

Nearly every other energy issue has been tied to CO_2 emissions, with policy proposals emanating from Washington DC and academia calling for government intervention.

Few if any proposals call for drilling in the outer continental shelf to alleviate dependence on foreign oil. Ostensibly because of concerns over oil spills, when actually it is because oil, when used as a fuel, emits CO_2.

The Controversy

Here is a sampling of proposals calling for government intervention.

- Impose tax penalties on those who buy cars not deemed fuel efficient by the government. Or alternatively, institute "Fee-bates" for those buying fuel efficient cars, paid for by penalty payments from those who buy fuel inefficient cars.

- Force States to impose higher license and registration fees for so-called gas guzzlers', as determined by government.

- Increase gasoline taxes.

- Scrap dirty cars earlier through creative financing so that people who couldn't afford to buy a car can buy a new, highly fuel efficient car. (Sound familiar?)

- Impose a $65 per barrel floor on the price of oil.

- Impose cap & trade regulations.

While some of these feel-good proposals are merely onerous, others are absurd.

Imposing a floor price on oil may sound good as a way to allow alternative energy companies to confidently plan their financing, but it is a bizarre proposal.

The only ways for this proposal to be implemented are:

1. Have the government buy the oil when the market price is below $65 and then resell it to the oil companies, pocketing the difference.

2. Have the oil companies pay the government the difference between the lower market price and the $65 floor.

3. Allow Saudi Arabia, Venezuela and other countries to sell their oil to the United States at $65 per barrel, while

13

selling it to China and other countries at the lower market price.

The first two alternatives are a hidden tax on consumers, while the third would be akin to joining OPEC.

Cap & trade regulations are equally absurd, as the following chapters will show.

Enacting cap & trade regulations if technologies do not exist to significantly cut CO2 could be a national disaster.

Once the genie is out of the bottle it will be difficult to put him back. What happens in a few years if Congress determines that CO2 emissions can't be cut? How do they unravel the actions that have been set in motion?

How, for example, will the market for CO2 credits or permits be shut down after trillions of dollars have been invested in them?

Shouldn't we be certain that technologies exist for cutting CO2 emissions before establishing cap & trade regulations?

Chapter 2

Proposed Congressional Action

Several bills have been introduced in Congress to establish cap & trade regulations. An attempt was made to bring the Warner-Lieberman bill out of committee, but the Senate leadership decided not to bring the bill to the floor for a vote in an election year when gasoline prices had skyrocketed.

The House passed the American Clean Energy and Security Act, HR2454 on June 26th, 2009, referred to as the Waxman-Markey cap & trade bill. It now goes to the Senate.

One of these bills, the Waxman-Markey or a Senate alternative, probably renamed and amended, will be debated and probably voted on in 2009.

With these regulations the emphasis is on cap, in cap & trade. There is nothing to trade if a cap hasn't been established for CO_2 emissions. Under this system a company would have to have a permit for every metric ton of CO_2 it emits. If it emits more CO_2 than it has permits, it must buy permits from companies having surplus permits.

A cap & trade system is viewed by many as a way to allow market forces to work. The 1990 Clean Air Act established a cap & trade system for SO_2 and it was viewed as a success.

Cap & trade bills that have been introduced in the Senate include bills by[3]:

- Sen. John Warner (R., Virginia.) and Sen. Joseph Lieberman (I., Conn.). Their bill is intended to reduce CO_2 emissions to 60% below 1990 emission levels by 2050. (This bill was originally the McCain – Lieberman bill.)

- Sen. Jeff Bingaman (D., N.M.) and Sen. Arlen Specter (R., PA). Their approach stabilizes emissions at their 2013 level by 2020 and 1990 levels by 2030. They include a "safety valve" requiring the government to issue additional permits if the price of permits rises too sharply.[4]

Proposed Congressional Action

- Sen. John Kerry (D., MA) and Sen. Olympia Snow (R., ME). Their bill would require a 60% reduction in CO2 emissions from 1990 levels by 2050.

- Sen. Bernard Sanders (I., VT) and Sen. Barbara Boxer (D., CA). Their bill would require an 80% reduction in CO2 emissions from 1990 levels by 2050.

These bills cover all sectors of the economy.

A bill introduced by Senators Diane Feinstein (D., CA) and Tom Carper (D., DE) targeted the electric generation sector.[5] This bill is so complicated it is difficult to calculate the amount electric utilities would have to reduce their CO2 emissions by 2050.

A rough estimate shows that the Feinstein-Carper bill would require a 30% reduction in CO2 emissions below 1990 levels from the Electric Sector by 2050.

The Warner-Lieberman bill was debated and defeated in 2008, however, this bill or one of the others or an entirely new bill is likely to be brought to the floor during 2009.

In October 2008, bill was introduced in the House by House Energy and Commerce Committee Chairman, John Dingell and Energy and Air Quality subcommittee Chairman, Rick Boucher. This 461 page bill requires cutting CO2 emissions 80% by 2050 by relying on cap & trade.

The Dingell-Boucher bill wasn't aggressive enough for the Democrat House leadership, and the leadership replaced Dingell with Waxman as chairman of the House Energy and Commerce Committee. The Dingell-Boucher bill was superseded by the Waxman-Markey bill that is over 1300 pages long after being amended at the last minute to insert compromises required to obtain congressional votes for its passage.

When the government establishes a cap on CO2 emissions it creates a scarcity, which creates value where none existed before. It's possible to call a cap & trade system a scam because there is no underlying value. Value is arbitrary and created by government. Government is influenced by lobbyists trying to gain an advantage for the industries they represent. The system is being gamed.

CO_2 permits will impose a cost on all sectors of the economy, including the residential sector where costs will ultimately be absorbed. How costs are imposed depends on whether the permits are allocated by the government (where they are initially free) or are purchased from the government in an auction. In the latter there is an immediate cost to industries etc.[6]

If the permits are auctioned, the government will receive an immediate huge infusion of cash. Congress can use these billions of dollars for any program it wants.

Is this how President Obama intends to pay for all his proposals? Or help placate Americans by giving people who don't pay income taxes additional tax credits to help offset the higher costs they will incur when companies raise their prices to cover the cost of the permits?

This is not a new idea. The paper "Well-Designed Climate Policies Can Generate the Resources Needed to Address Crucial Policies" itemizes how receipts from cap & trade will be apportioned, with monies going to hold low income families harmless and to provide relief to middle income families.[7]

This admonition about having to reimburse poor families is tacit admission that cap & trade legislation will result in a huge hidden tax increase, by raising the cost of nearly everything Americans purchase.

The Waxman-Markey bill includes these payments which is proof that cap & trade will increase energy costs for all Americans.

If permits are allocated, any immediate cost will depend on how they are allocated. Those who receive too few permits will have to purchase permits from those who receive more permits than they need to cover their CO_2 emissions.

Proposed Congressional Action

Bureaucrats in government will establish caps for each industry, thereby determining whether an industry receives sufficient permits to cover its emissions.

Each year (or some other period established by the government) caps will be lowered so that industries will have increasingly lower levels of permitted CO_2 emissions. If industries do not have permits to cover their emissions over the cap, they will have to purchase permits from industries that have excess permits.

As industries buy permits they will incur costs. These costs will increase as the caps are lowered and will be passed on to consumers in the form of higher prices. The Congressional Budget Office said that companies would raise prices even if the credits issued to companies were free because companies would factor the cost of using the credits versus selling them to another company for a profit.

This is what happened in Germany when the largest German utility, RWE, charged customers for the emission permits even though they had been received free from the government. The reason given by RWE was that even though they were free, they still had economic value.[8]

An individual company or utility can invest in new equipment to lower its emissions in order to remain within its lowered cap. This also increases costs unless there is a cost savings (through improved efficiency) over and above the savings from not having to buy permits.

This assumes, of course, that new technologies are available for decreasing CO_2 emissions. *This is a very dangerous assumption.*

Industries will recover all of their increased costs by increasing prices. In the final analysis, it is the consumer who will pay the bill.

It is clear from the above that there is room to game the system and create inequities.

Proposed Congressional Action

For example, DuPont wants to receive credit for past reductions in CO_2 emissions. If they get permits for actions they took in the past, they will have permits they can sell.

The electric utility industry wants economy wide caps, including CAFE standards. The automobile industry wants the burden to be borne by utilities.

Utilities that generate electricity using nuclear power want permits allocated based on the amount of electricity generated. This would give them excess permits that could be sold. Other utilities want the caps based on the amount of CO_2 emitted. In this instance, the nuclear power companies would receive few if any permits.

Or caps could be established based on the most recent year: Or based on an average number of years. Companies that have invested in new equipment or processes would want the cap based on an average over the preceding years rather than the most recent year.

Manufacturers may want to secure credit for the energy saving reductions from the appliances they make. Lower energy use by a refrigerator could accrue to the manufacturer making the new refrigerator. The same could be true for air conditioning units, ranges, computers, TV's etc.

Individual states will lobby Congress to obtain higher caps for their industries or credits for manufacturers in their state.

As pointed out by Power Magazine, "complying with GHG limits would be far more costly for low-emission utilities than for big CO_2 producers, penalizing the former group and rewarding the latter." High emission utilities will be able to invest to reduce their emissions while low emitters will find it difficult to reduce their emissions. High emitters would obtain permits for their reductions; permits they could sell. Low emitting utilities will have fewer opportunities to reduce their emissions to obtain salable permits.

Jim Rogers, CEO of Duke Power, who was once with ENRON, has been hypocritical about cap & trade legislation. When it appeared as though carbon permits would be issued free, without charge, he was in favor of cap & trade legislation. When it appeared more likely that carbon permits would be auctioned and that companies will have to pay for them, he no longer favored cap & trade legislation. Or more precisely, he doesn't favor cap & trade legislation with which he doesn't agree.

When carbon permits are given freely to companies, they can use them to fatten their bottom line by selling the ones they don't need. When they have to pay for carbon permits it hurts their bottom line, unless they can foist the costs onto their customers.

Coal producing states will want caps established at the point of usage, not at the point of origin. Coal producing states, like West Virginia, Pennsylvania and Wyoming, will pressure their Senators on this issue.

Some states with forests may want to receive credit for the CO_2 absorbed by their trees.

Some groups will want the automobile manufacturers to meet tail pipe emission standards as being proposed in Europe. In this instance manufacturers who produce small cars will have an advantage over manufacturers producing large cars.

Lobbyists in Washington DC will earn huge salaries for lobbying Congress to produce legislation favorable to the industry they represent.

The **average consumer will have very little say** in these negotiations or the legislation produced by Congress.

Financial businesses will be big winners with a cap & trade system as they will be able to buy and sell permits. Think, ENRON on steroids.

Shortly after the collapse of the financial markets some of the world's leading investment bankers met in London to explore how they could "cash in" on carbon. Their meeting examined how

Proposed Congressional Action

"investment banks can profit today from an increasingly diverse range of carbon-related investment opportunities" with an examination of "hybrid and complex carbon credit structured products", "derivative/synthetic carbon products", and "sub-index arbitrage strategies".[9]

We should all be concerned if leading bankers are hovering over carbon credits like vultures.

Unless the cap & trade system is adopted worldwide, it is very likely that manufacturers will move their plants to foreign countries to avoid the added cost of buying permits. This will mean the further loss of jobs. If developing countries such as China and India do not cap their CO_2 emissions, worldwide CO_2 emissions will increase even if the U.S. reduces its CO_2 emissions.

By one estimate, China's CO_2 emissions will increase by 60% over the next decade.

A feature of the Kyoto Treaty is the Clean Development Mechanism allowing companies to purchase credits, or invest in projects that reduce CO_2 emissions, in foreign countries.

But there is tremendous suspicion about the veracity of CO_2 emissions claimed by foreign countries. It has also been pointed out by Stanford University's Michael Wara that billions are being spent by EU companies to buy credits based on CO_2 emission reductions in foreign countries and that the EU is overpaying for credits. There is some evidence that companies in developing countries are gaming the system by purposely increasing CO_2 emissions where it's easy to cut them later, and then selling credits to European countries.

While Europe is a prime example of how these credits are being misused, it's not necessary to look at the EU and its experience with the Clean Development Mechanism to see how the system can be gamed.

The sale of climate credits in the U.S. is already being gamed.

21

Proposed Congressional Action

Trash dumps, from Pennsylvania to North Dakota, with previously installed systems for capturing methane (a greenhouse gas) are now selling carbon credits on the Chicago Climate Exchange.[10]

Selling climate credits is supposed to be reserved for those situations where projects would not otherwise have been initiated, but are undertaken as the result of the financial incentive afforded by selling carbon credits. In many instances the dumps now selling carbon credits installed methane capturing systems several years ago because methane could be sold to local utilities. There was no need for the carbon credits.

If foreign countries refuse to join a worldwide cap & trade system to cap their emissions, C. Boyden Gray, US ambassador to the European Union, said retaliatory steps could be taken against China and India. Rep. Rick Boucher (D., VA.) suggested requiring countries who don't cap their emissions to purchase credits from the U.S. in order to export goods into the United States.

The Waxman-Markey bill includes this type of language that could result in a trade war.

These threats are similar to those made by the European Union against the U.S.

The complexity of a worldwide cap & trade system is mind-boggling. How will it affect world trade? Will cap & trade legislation become another disaster like Smoot-Hawley?

These are some of the reasons why many economists believe that a carbon tax is preferable to cap & trade regulations. But foreign countries haven't shown any inclination to accept carbon taxes.

Mr. David Wyss at Standard & Poor's Corporation, summarized the alternative approaches by saying, "A tax puts pressure on the market, rather than forcing an artificial solution on it.[11]

With either a cap & trade system or a carbon tax, the average consumer will pay the bill.

22

Chapter 3

U.S. CO2 Emissions

The U.S. Energy Information Administration tracks CO2 emissions and publishes a report annually showing the source of CO2 emissions. See Table I.

- The generation of electricity accounts for 39% of all CO2 emissions in the United States.

- Gasoline, primarily from powering automobiles and light trucks (SUV's), accounts for 20% of all U.S. CO2 emissions.

- Industrial emissions accounted for 18% of total U.S. CO2 emissions. Within the Industrial Sector, manufacturing accounted for approximately 84% of Industrial emissions[12] (or 12% of total U.S. CO2 emissions). Agriculture, forestry, fishing, construction and mining accounted for the rest of the industrial sector's CO2 emissions.

- Transportation other than gasoline accounted for 13% of total U.S. CO2 emissions. These emissions came primarily from heavy trucks, locomotives, ships and jet fuel.

- The residential sector accounted for 6% of total U.S. CO2 emissions. Space heating and appliances accounted for these CO2 emissions.

- The commercial sector represents 4% of total U.S. CO2 emissions. These emissions came mostly from space heating (primarily natural gas) from office buildings, shopping malls, schools and hospitals.

(Lighting and air conditioning emissions from the Residential and Commercial Sectors due to electricity are included in the Electric Sector.)

U.S. CO2 Emissions 2004		
Source	MMT	% Total
Electric Generation	2298.6	39%
Gasoline	1162.6	20%
Industrial	1069.3	18%
Transportation (Excluding Gasoline)	771.1	13%
Residential	374.7	6%
Commercial	228.8	4%
United States Total	5905.1	100%

Table I

Total excludes approximately 70 MMT of CO2 emissions from miscellaneous sources.

Source: *Emission of Greenhouse Gasses in the United States 2005* by DOE Energy Information Administration.

MMT = Million Metric Tons   1 Metric Ton = 2205 pounds

Some non government organizations have championed major cuts in CO2 emissions. The Natural Resources Defense Council supports an 80% reduction in CO2 emissions from 1990 levels by 2050. The EU has proposed a 50% reduction from 1990 levels.[13] The United Nations also endorses an 80% reduction for the U.S. so that developing countries, such as China and India, can continue to increase their CO2 emissions, but at a slower rate of increase. The Liberal Democrats of the U.K. have suggested it might be necessary to reduce CO2 emissions by an amount approaching 100% by 2050.[14]

U.S. CO2 Emissions

The year 1990 is frequently used as the bench mark against which reductions in CO2 are measured. The Kyoto Protocol was established in 1990 and is a convenient reference point.

Confusion can be generated when the media reports on carbon rather than CO2 emissions.

Tonnes carbon can be converted to tonnes CO2 by multiplying tonnes carbon by 3.67.

The phrase "common but differentiated responsibilities" is included in treaties and agreements.[15] It has been interpreted by many to indicate that developed countries (e.g., the U.S.) should provide financial or technical support to developing countries to assist them in cutting their CO2 emissions.[16] In other words, the U.S. taxpayer should help pay China and India to reduce their emissions. Another interpretation is that there is a common responsibility to reduce CO2 emissions, but that each country can have different targets.

Table II, with the accompanying chart, shows U.S. CO2 emission levels by sector that would have to be achieved for the U.S. to reduce CO2 emissions by 80% below 1990 levels.

As seen in Chapter 1:

- Proposed Congressional legislation requires cuts in CO2 emissions of up to 80% below 1990 levels.
- The EPA is poised to implement regulations requiring an 80% cut in CO2 emissions.

A cursory glance at Table II and the accompanying chart, immediately raises the question as to whether it is even possible, let alone desirable, to achieve these huge reductions.

Three issues impact whether it's possible to cut CO2 emissions by 80% or 60%. Or by any significant amount?

1. Are there replacement technologies available that result in substantial reductions in CO2 emissions?

25

2. Is there the political will to adopt these technologies?

3. Can conservation achieve the legislated targets?

80% Reduction in U.S. CO2 Emissions from 1990 levels by 2050 (in MMT).		
Source	2004 Actual	2050Target 80% below 1990
Electric Generation	2298.6	360.6
Gasoline	1162.6	191.0
Industrial	1069.3	212.7
Transportation (Excluding Gasoline)	771.1	122.9
Residential	374.7	67.9
Commercial	228.8	44.7
United States Total	5905.1	999.9

Table II

Total excludes approximately 70 MMT of CO2 emissions from miscellaneous sources.

Source: *Emission of Greenhouse Gasses in the United States 2005* by DOE Energy Information Administration.

MMT = Million Metric Tons

Various interest groups tout specific solutions that get trumpeted in the press. Some that have received wide dissemination include; wind power, compact fluorescent lighting, biomass, solar, smart buildings, and nuclear power.

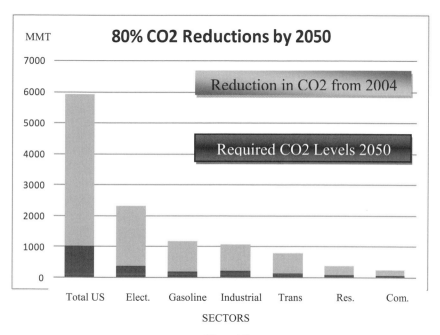

Chart I

In addition to the above three issues, there is the very real problem of a growing population and the effect it will have on U.S. CO2 emissions.

The Census Bureau estimates that the U.S. population in 2050 will be 420 million. This is an increase of 139 million from the 2000 census. This increase of 139 million happens to equal the total population of the United States during WWII.

U.S. CO2 Emissions

The U.S. population in 2050 is therefore forecast to increase by 49% from 2000. These additional Americans will want to heat and light their homes, use air conditioning and drive automobiles. *They will also want jobs.*

The increased population will result in more CO2 emissions and make it even more difficult for the U.S. to achieve the 2050 CO2 emission targets.

The enormity of the challenge is made clear by the following two observations.

1. Current U.S. per capita CO2 emissions are 20.5 tons. An 80% reduction will result in per capita emissions of 2.4 tons in 2050.

2. An 80% reduction will lower CO2 emissions to around the levels they were during World War I, during the presidency of Woodrow Wilson.

   There were few cars during the presidency of Woodrow Wilson; most people still relied on horses and carriages for transportation. Commercial air travel was still the dream of people like Eddie Rickenbacker and Juan Trippe. Many people still cooked using wooden stoves. There weren't any washing machines or clothes driers. The ice man delivered ice twice each week so that people could keep their food cold.

It should be noted that it will be easier for Europe to achieve its targets as its population growth could be negative. European population could decline from 375 million in 2000 to fewer than 300 million by 2050 if present trends continue.[17] This projection doesn't include immigration which could offset much of the decline.

While demands for electricity and automobiles will increase in the United States, demand for these items in Europe will decline or remain unchanged. Europe's pronouncements about what the U.S. should do to cut its CO2 emissions should be viewed in this light.

28

Chapter 4

Slippery Slope

The skids were greased in 1990 at the United Nations Conference on Environment and Development (UNCED) at Rio de Janeiro, also called the Earth Summit. It was an election year and Al Gore had just published his book Earth in the Balance. President George H.W. Bush was President and, after taking considerable political heat from Al Gore, attended the conference.

Delegates from 172 countries attended the conference, including 108 heads of State. There were 2,400 representatives from non-governmental organizations (NGO's) with some 17,000 people attending a parallel NGO forum.

The conference established the United Nations Framework Convention on Climate Change (UNFCCC). This treaty was signed by President G. H. W. Bush and quickly ratified by the Senate.

These events took place under the pressure of a political campaign.

Presumably the Senate ratified the treaty assuming it was a hollow document where all the actions required by the treaty were voluntary.

Unfortunately, the UNFCCC established a bureaucratic structure that would always force the United States into a corner.

The treaty established that each country would have a single vote, thus leaving the United States at the mercy of approximately 185 countries, many of whom have agenda's opposing the United States.

There is no veto so the United States is consistently outvoted.

The UNFCCC also established a Conference of the Parties (COP) where all the signatories would hold annual meetings. Similar to the Earth Summit in Rio, these meetings are attended by the approximately 185 signatory countries under the auspices of the United Nations. Many NGO's attend the COP meetings where they play an active, but nonvoting, role. There were over 10,000 participants at the December 2007, COP 13 in Bali, Indonesia.

29

Slippery Slope

The most recent manifestation of this voting arrangement was at the COP 13 meeting in Bali, where the participants booed the American delegation because it didn't want to agree to the Bali Road Map. Fearing negative publicity from the news media the American delegation succumbed to the "consensus."

As a group, these countries have nothing to lose by placing demands on the United States as they can easily outvote the U.S. on every issue.

The COP acts as judge and jury with respect to climate change issues and has established subsidiary bodies for this purpose, specifically the Subsidiary Body for Implementation (SBI) and the Subsidiary Body for Scientific and Technological Advice (SBSTA).

These groups hold meetings more frequently than COP meetings and NGO's are also allowed to participate in them.

There is a provision for reconciling disputes but resolution is through the International Court of Justice, arbitration or conciliation by a group appointed from among the 185 member parties. In essence, the United States places itself under the jurisdiction of parties who inherently are not sympathetic toward the United States.

Parties to the UNFCCC should act "on the basis of equity, and in accordance with their differentiated responsibilities and respective capabilities."

Article 4.4 states that "developed country parties ... shall assist developing country parties that are particularly vulnerable to the adverse affect of climate change in meeting costs of adaptation to those adverse affects."

This theme is repeated throughout the UNFCCC where developed countries (especially the United States) should bear the burden of reducing CO_2 emissions and also provide financial support to developing countries.

Slippery Slope

The UNFCCC also established a requirement for preparing "educational materials and creating public awareness on climate change and its effects," which amounts to self-promotion and pre-empts arguments to the contrary.

The language of the UNFCCC is frequently imprecise, and this has serious implications for the United States. Under the Convention, parties have "the responsibility to ensure that activities within their jurisdiction or control do not cause damage to the environment of other States or of areas beyond the limits of national jurisdiction."

Who is to say whether emissions from American factories are causing damage to the environment of Europe or any other area of the world? At the very least, this statement allows people to pillory the United States because, in their minds, the United States is harming the environment.

Terms such as "sustainable development", "sustainable economic growth", and "sustainable agriculture" are not defined in the Convention. Presumably COP meetings or SBI or SBSTA meetings will make determinations about these terms and the United States will have little to say about how they will be administered.

The UNFCCC was supposed to be voluntary, but has been used to pressure the United States. The Kyoto protocol that emerged from the UNFCCC was legally binding and dropped all pretense of volunteerism.

It was signed on behalf of the United States by Al Gore.

It established legally binding emission targets for developed countries, listed in Annex I of the UNFCCC. The United States was to reduce its greenhouse gas emissions by 7% from 1990 levels, but the United States never ratified the Kyoto Treaty.

Annex II countries, including the United States if it had ratified the treaty, were obligated to provide funding and insurance to developing countries; including obligations for any perceived impacts on

31

Slippery Slope

developing countries from actions taken by Annex I countries in meeting their emission targets under the Kyoto protocol.

India and China are not Annex I or II countries so are not required to meet any target for reducing greenhouse gasses and are considered developing countries under the Convention and Kyoto Protocol.

Continuing the bureaucratic nature of the Convention and the Kyoto Protocol, the COP would serve as the Meeting of the Parties, "COP/MOP" for the Kyoto Protocol.

Today, the EU is still struggling to meet its required 5% reduction in greenhouse gas emissions, even though the base year of 1990 gave Europe a tremendous advantage. The collapse of East Germany's industries and the UK's transitioning to North Sea natural gas automatically resulted in large reductions in emissions. Most recently, EU emissions have been increasing.

The Bali Road Map established in December 2007, created a process that would culminate in Copenhagen, Denmark where the "fifteenth session of the Conference of the Parties and the fifth session of the COP/MOP shall be held from November 30 to December 12, 2009" to arrive at a new treaty to replace the Kyoto Protocol.[18]

Since the meeting in Bali, there have been a series of COP meetings taking place to prepare for the meeting in Copenhagen, Denmark where the Bali Road Map is to reach fruition with a new treaty requiring reductions in worldwide emissions of 50% by 2050.

As noted earlier, the United Nations is demanding that developed countries, including the United States, cut their emissions 80% by 2050. China and India have repeatedly said they will not agree to emission targets.

Having ratified the UNFCCC the United States must participate in the Copenhagen meeting where it will be under tremendous pressure to agree to whatever emerges from Copenhagen in 2009

Slippery Slope

President Obama will appoint the American delegation and provide it with instructions. President Obama has said he strongly favors cutting CO2 emissions 80% by 2050 and that he wants the United States to assume a leadership role in this regard.

Will President Obama sign a new treaty, perhaps known as the Copenhagen Protocol, legally binding the United States to dramatic cuts in CO2 emissions? And will a liberal Senate ratify the treaty?

Chapter 5

Europe's Cap & Trade Experience

Europe adopted a cap & trade system in 2005. Some American politicians have visited Europe to examine Europe's program.

The European Union (EU) began its cap & trade system, or carbon market, by establishing quotas for CO_2 emissions for its member states. Unfortunately, the quotas were set too high creating a glut of CO_2 credits (permits) which caused the price for CO_2 credits to collapse.

Now, in an effort to correct its initial mistake, the EU is attempting to tighten the quotas for each state in the next round of its cap & trade system.

This has led to the poorer new member states, which already have low per capita CO_2 emissions, being assigned even lower emission quotas.

Latvia is typical of the new EU states that were formerly part of the Soviet Union. Latvia has the lowest per capita greenhouse gas emissions in the EU, yet the EU is attempting to force Latvia to cut its proposed emissions by around 50%.

This could force Latvia to buy credits from older EU members who have done little to meet their Kyoto targets. (Most of the 12 new EU members are meeting their Kyoto targets.)

Development of new projects may shift from Latvia to foreign countries that do not impose restrictions on CO_2 emissions. Not only will worldwide CO_2 emissions continue unchecked but additional CO_2 emissions will occur when the goods are transported back to Europe.

The EU is attempting to have carbon emission credits auctioned beginning in 2013. This will hurt those Eastern European counties who use coal to generate electricity. Poland, for example, derives 95% of its electricity from coal and believes its electricity prices will increase by 70% if it must buy carbon credits at auction.[19]

Europe's Cap & Trade Experience

The ability of new EU members (such as Czech Republic, Latvia and Lithuania) to grow their economies is being "impaired because they lack the resources to confront the massive <u>business lobbies</u> of the EU's most developed and richest countries."

The system is being gamed at the expense of the little person.

The EU also allows businesses to buy credits from foreign countries (e.g., China and India) to help them meet their targets. Obviously this won't reduce Europe's CO2 emissions. It also gives richer companies an advantage over smaller companies in Eastern Europe.

Then there is the proposal to include forests in the trading scheme. Under the proposal, "forests and other land would be credited as stores of carbon, allowing landowners to sell the resulting permits" to factories that emit CO2. But what happens if forest fires or drought release the CO2 stored in the forests. Permits would have been issued for CO2 that wasn't stored safely in trees.[20]

The new EU members have sued the EU over the emission standards being imposed on them by the EU.[21]

The EU adopted a different approach than the U.S. for reducing CO2 emissions from automobiles. The EU is proposing tail pipe standards for cars by limiting cars to 130 grams of CO2 per km by 2012. For comparison the Mercedes M-Class's CO2 output is 249 grams per kilometer, while the average for European car manufacturers is 161. This is pitting France and Italy that make small cars, against Germany that makes large cars like the Mercedes and BMW.

Imposition of caps on industry and utilities is increasing costs and the consumer is paying the price.

In spite of all these efforts to establish a cap & trade system, the EU has not been able to reduce its CO2 emissions over the past few years. EU emissions increased 1 – 1.5% in 2006.[22]

Europe's Cap & Trade Experience

Congressional White Paper

A White Paper issued by the U.S. Congress' Committee on Energy and Commerce[23] acknowledges the problems associated with cap & trade regulations.

The Congressional paper discusses where the "point of control" for CO_2 emissions should be placed: Upstream, Downstream or Midstream. They describe the complexities surrounding emissions from automobiles; a downstream point of regulation complicated by the millions of individual emission sources. The White Paper suggests it is best to regulate emissions at the upstream source which are the refineries.

The White Paper fails, however, to examine the realities of controlling Transportation Sector emissions.

The point of regulation the White Paper seems to prefer is the refineries and importers. Refineries, however, do not control how much gasoline is used. Gasoline usage is controlled by millions of individual drivers. The only way refineries could control emissions from automobiles is by raising the price of gasoline to astronomic levels or by refusing to produce gasoline. Neither option is realistic.

Alternatively, the "point of control" could be the manufacturer of automobiles. Here, the government could mandate that only certain cars could be sold in the U.S.: For example, only those cars that achieve 100 mpg of gasoline or diesel fuel. (Or impose a cap that accomplishes the same objective.) By one estimate, 100 mpg is required for there to be any significant reduction in gasoline usage.[24]

Or the government could impose gasoline rationing to control emissions from the source if the downstream "point of control" is selected.

While the complexities of the Transportation Sector are obvious, the same issues surround the Commercial and Residential Sectors.

37

Europe's Cap & Trade Experience

The Waxman-Markey bill addresses the residential issue by requiring new and existing homes to be audited to determine whether they meet energy standards.

Waxman-Markey establishes the Retrofit for Energy and Environmental Performance (REEP) program that addresses both residential and commercial buildings.

Section 202 includes the following: "The Administrator shall develop and implement, in consultation with the Secretary of Energy, standards for a national energy and environmental building retrofit policy for single-family and multifamily residences."

Waxman-Markey mandates that States must adhere to REEP if they are to receive funds from the program. In essence, all homeowners will likely have to adhere to the standards established by the federal government

If they don't meet these standards, homeowners who want to sell their homes will have to spend their money to meet the government's determined acceptable energy standard.

Chapter 6

Developing Countries

The G-77 is a block of 130 developing countries that urge developed countries to accept the burden of reducing CO2 emissions.

Speaking on behalf of G-77, Pakistani Environment Minister Syed Faisal Saleh Hayat said "rich countries should deepen their reduction commitments in the next phase of the Kyoto Protocol and also help poorer nations tackle impact of climate change."

China and India are the largest of the developing countries and they have repeatedly said they will not adopt fixed commitments for reducing CO2 emissions.

China passed the United States as the largest emitter of CO2 in 2009. India says it has only one fourth the per capita emissions as China and should be viewed differently.

All the developing countries cite the principle of "common but differentiated responsibilities"

All place the onus on the United States and other rich countries to cut CO2 emissions.

China is demanding that developed countries pay 1% of their GDP to developing countries, including China. This demand is a precondition to China agreeing to any plan for cutting CO2 emissions.

For the Group of Seven developed countries it would amount to over $300 billion.

For the United States, it would amount to more than $130 billion of taxpayer money.

Gao Guangsheng, head of the climate change office at the National Reform and Development Commission, China's main planning body, said that this "might not be enough."[25]

The money would be used to buy technology and equipment for cutting CO2 emissions.

39

Developing Countries

So, not only will U.S. taxpayers have to shoulder the burden of billions of hidden taxes with the enactment of cap & trade legislation, they must also fork over billions more to China and the other developing countries.

If we don't, China has said it won't agree to any program for cutting CO_2 emissions.

Some could call this "blackmail".

Indian Prime Minister Manmohan Singh joined in when he said "western nations haven't lived up to their commitment for technology transfer and additional financing since the Rio Conference." This is a reference to the principle of "common but differentiated responsibilities" ensconced in the United Nations Framework Convention on Climate Change agreed to in Rio and ratified by the Senate.

This commitment might come as a surprise to most American tax payers.

China is reportedly opening two new coal fired power plants each week.

Chinese Foreign Minister Yang Jiechi said "climate change is ultimately an issue of development and can only be resolved through development."

China has also taken the position that it has become the "Factory" for the world. It points out that developed countries have exported their CO_2 belching factories to China and that China should not be expected to set a target for cutting CO_2 when China is merely doing the rich countries' dirty work.

If China grows at 10% per year (approximately the rate of current growth) China's economy will double in 7 years. Presumably, CO_2 emissions will also double.

Developing Countries

India's Finance Minister P Chidambaram said, "India, being an energy deficient country, is obliged to explore every option available to produce and procure energy."

Sunita Narain, an Indian environmentalist told Reuters, "With climate change, we are looking at sharing the resources of the world and we are looking at *bringing some justice in the way they are distributed* -- so the rich world has to reduce its emissions so that the poor world can increase theirs." (Emphasis added. The quote has a familiar ring, dating back to Russia in 1918.)[26]

What this infers is that U.S. citizens should become poorer while India's citizens become richer.

Carbon Folly suggests it is better to adopt policies where everyone becomes richer.

At this writing, it is clear that developing countries do not intend to adopt fixed targets for cutting CO2.

The U.S. Energy Information Administration estimates that by 2010, developing countries will emit 20% more CO2 than the developed countries.

What is the outcome if developing countries refuse to cut their CO2 emissions while the United States forges ahead with cap & trade regulations?

One must wonder about China's motives when China refuses to cut its emissions while demanding the United States cuts its emissions. Perhaps the question is unfair, but where will the world be with a powerful China and a weak United States?

Chapter 7

Should I Be Concerned?

President Obama has said, "My presidency will mark a new chapter in America's leadership on climate change."

He said, "[I] will start with a federal cap and trade system. We will establish strong annual targets that set us on a course to reduce emissions to their 1990 levels by 2020 and reduce them an additional 80% by 2050."[27]

He has also said, referring to the United Nations negotiations to impose CO2 cuts on America, "you can be sure that the United States will once again engage vigorously in these negotiations, and help lead the world toward a new era of global cooperation on climate change."

How will cap & trade regulations or carbon taxes affect Americans?

These regulations will impose massive control over the lives of Americans, such as imposing restrictions on the size of their homes, restrictions on air travel, determining the kind of car they may own without paying a penalty, control of their thermostats to limit usage of air conditioning, and even how they cut their lawns.

They will require an immense bureaucracy to implement, manage and enforce the regulations.

These regulations will be Orwellian in scope and profoundly change America.

What if each American was given a plastic card containing their carbon allowance? Each time there was a transaction the card would be debited for the carbon usage resulting from the transaction. Filling the gas tank would debit the card for the CO2 caused by the amount of gasoline purchased. Lamb chops would debit the card for the green house gasses caused by sheep. Buying an airplane ticket would debit the card for the CO2 released by the jet engines.

Preposterous?

Should I Be Concerned?

Not quite. This scheme was suggested for the United Kingdom under a *Climate Change Bill.*

The Daily Mail reported:

> "One method could be personal carbon-allowances, where everyone is given a fixed amount of carbon to use each year. Each time they travel in a plane, buy petrol, go shopping or eat out would be recorded on a plastic card. The more frugal could sell spare carbon to those who want to indulge themselves. But if you were to run out of your carbon allowance, you could be barred from flying or driving."[28]

Perhaps cap & trade regulations proposed by Congress won't reach such an absurd outcome, but what could be the result of cap & trade regulations currently proposed by Congress or the regulations being proposed by the EPA?

Gasoline accounts for 20% of all U.S. CO2 emissions.

The simplest way to reduce CO2 emissions from gasoline is to restrict the use of gasoline. This could easily be accomplished with rationing.

Those who remember their history will remember the A and B stickers displayed on car windshields during WWII. The A sticker entitled the driver to 3 or 4 gallons of gas a week. Three gallons a week might approximate an 80% cut in gasoline usage.

How far can the average person drive each week on 3 gallons?

Ridiculous?

Maybe not, since there are no other alternatives currently available that will result in an 80% reduction in CO2 emissions from gasoline. (See Part Two for discussion of nuclear energy.)

Americans take electricity for granted. Need light? Flick the light switch. Want food to keep? Put it in a refrigerator run by electricity.

Should I Be Concerned?

Want air conditioning? Turn on the air conditioning unit run by electricity. Want Heat? Turn on the furnace whose blower is run by electricity.

Factories cannot operate without electricity. No electricity—no jobs.

Shutting down all coal fired power generation plants would cut CO2 emissions from electricity by the required amount—but would only cut total U.S. emissions by about a third.

Shutting down all coal fired power plants would eliminate half of all electricity generated in the U.S.

Some cities and states are already trying to prohibit the construction of coal fired power plants. Some are trying to close existing coal fired power plants.

A court has ruled that the EPA must consider whether the best available control technology (BACT) to limit carbon dioxide emissions under the Clean Air Act should be required before issuing permits for new coal plants. This ruling could delay the construction of new coal plants, and stop construction if the EPA decides that BACT are required.[29]

Dr. James Hansen, head of NASA's Goddard Institute for Space Studies, has called for closing coal fired power plants.

Absurd? Yes. But not if there were ways to generate electricity without using coal. Nuclear power could result in more electricity without emitting CO2. Wind and other renewables could generate a miniscule amount of additional electricity.

Without building 350 new nuclear power plants the following scenario is probable if all coal fired power plants are shut down. There is no technology except nuclear that can replace all existing coal fired power plants while cutting CO2 emissions by 80%. And CO2 emissions can't be cut by 80% without shutting down the coal

Should I Be Concerned?

fired power plants. (See Chapter 8 – Coal, for information on Carbon Capture and Sequestration.)

Remember the blackouts in WWII? Or the blackouts that have occurred from time to time when the electric transmission system failed?

America would go dark at night and resemble the America of WWII with its blackouts after cap & trade regulations have been imposed on its citizens and the regulations start to force the closing of coal fired power plants.

Here are some actions that would have to be taken when half of America's electricity production is shut down.

- Eliminate all street lighting, except for traffic signals.

- Eliminate all outdoor electric signs such as for advertising.

- Have stores cut most of their lighting to allow only enough light for safety. (No display lighting.)

- Limit all stores and restaurants (grocery, department, cleaners, drug, etc.) to operating during daylight hours only.

- Grocery stores could cut their refrigeration dramatically by only carrying one brand of ice cream and one brand of frozen dinners. (Better yet, prohibit frozen foods as they are unnecessary.)

- Shut down all escalators.

- Meter homes so as to limit the amount of electricity they consume. This would include dramatic reductions in the use of electric dryers. (Cloths could be hung outdoors to dry. Most people hung out their cloths to dry in the first half of the twentieth century. This included during the winter when cloths became cardboard stiff when hung outdoors.)

Should I Be Concerned?

- Limit the use of residential air conditioning to when temperatures exceed 90^0 F. This could be accomplished by installing smart meters where the electric utility can control the thermostat in a person's home or apartment. This was proposed in California.[30]

- Eliminate air conditioning in stores and movie theaters. (Americans survived without air-conditioning before the 1930's.)

- Establish rolling blackouts.

- Limit the hours of operation for factories.

- Limit the hours of operation for the Internet as computers and the Internet consume large amounts of electricity.

- Limit the hours of TV usage and prohibit energy hogging flat panel displays.

Rich Americans could install solar panels on their roofs so they could avoid the prohibition on air-conditioning and use of electricity in their homes. The middle class and poor, and those who lived in cities would be out of luck.

Preposterous? Maybe so, but not if all coal fired power plants are shut down and nuclear plants aren't built to replace them. The next chapter explains in detail why these outcomes are realistic—and probable.

These are the lifestyle changes that must occur with cap & trade regulations with the current state of technologies. The changes won't happen all at once but will evolve over a decade or so. At first utilities will buy CO2 credits, but the cost of credits will become exorbitant after several years and utilities will opt to shut their coal fired power plants.

47

Should I Be Concerned?

If utilities are given free permits they can delay shutting down their coal fired power plants; but free permits are a scam to get votes to pass the legislation, as was the case with House passage of Waxman-Markey HR 24554. Once cap & trade is established, free permits will be abolished and utilities will be forced to buy permits.

This is what has happened in Europe where free permits were originally issued. CO_2 emissions weren't cut so Europe is now forcing companies to buy their permits.

Most areas of the country have excess generating capacity of around eight to ten percent. Utilities plan for this excess capacity to absorb sudden overloads which can occur on exceptionally hot or cold days. This excess capacity will be the first to disappear and the public won't notice it until a sudden overload exists and the system shuts down causing a blackout.

The economic outcome is likely to be draconian. No electricity— No jobs.

As dramatic as these outcomes seem, they will be <u>unavoidable</u> if cap & trade regulations are enacted by Congress or the EPA <u>before</u> technologies are developed that allow for continued generation of electricity and continued use of cars and other necessities, such as air conditioning and refrigeration.

Current legislation merely <u>assume</u> technologies exist that will allow for reducing CO_2 emissions by 80%. There are technologies, but, other than nuclear for generating electricity, <u>they do not yet exist</u>, except in theory.

For example, not a single power plant has been built in the United States that captures CO_2. NOT ONE. Not a single power plant has been retrofitted to capture CO_2. NOT ONE.

Yet all the proposed bills assume these technologies are already available.

PART TWO

Part two examines whether there are proven alternatives for achieving an 80% cut in CO2 emissions. Or for achieving any significant reduction in CO2 emissions.

Alternatives for generating electricity are examined in Chapter 8. Alternatives for reducing gasoline usage are examined in Chapter 9. Other Sectors are examined in Chapter 10.

Chapter 8

Alternatives for Generating Electricity

Generating electricity accounts for 39% of total U.S. CO2 emissions. (See Table I)

Coal currently accounts for nearly half of the electricity generated in the U.S.; Nuclear accounts for 20%; Natural gas for 21% and Hydro for 7%. (Oil currently accounts for less than 2% of total electricity generation.)[31]

Coal accounts for 82% of CO2 emissions from the generation of electricity, i.e., 32% of total U.S. CO2 emissions.

Natural gas accounts for 13% of CO2 emissions from the generation of electricity, i.e., 5% of total U.S. CO2 emissions.

Nuclear

It would seem that nuclear power, that emits zero CO2, would be the natural choice for reducing CO2 emissions from the generation of electricity.

Alternatives for Generating Electricity

Two obstacles stand in the way of achieving any significant reductions in CO_2 emissions from nuclear power.

1. Expiring operating licenses.

2. Political will.

There are 104 nuclear power plants in the U.S. Most of these have already received a 20 year extension to their operating licenses, and all the remaining nuclear plants are expected to also receive 20 year extensions in spite of lawsuits.

As a result of these extensions, all 104 nuclear plants can continue to operate until the expiration of their updated licenses.

There is a question as to how many of these nuclear power plants will receive a second extension to their operating license. Some will probably receive extensions, but others will not.

At issue will be the design life of the plants. How reliable is the piping and wiring of an 80 year old nuclear plant? More important, what will be the condition of reactor vessels due to neutron flux embrittlement? (Embrittlement of the reactor vessel can be likened to a plastic container that is originally tough and flexible, that over time becomes brittle like a glass container.)

As a result, an unknown number of nuclear power plants may have to be shut down by 2053. Some may have to be shut down beginning in 2029, and more may have to be shut down during the 2030's.

Unless all the shuttered plants are replaced over the next fifty years, the percentage of electricity produced by nuclear power will decline.

The only alternative to nuclear power for base load use, is coal or oil. Building new coal fired plants to replace nuclear plants will increase CO_2 emissions. Not building new power plants to replace the shuttered nuclear plants will result in a shortage of electricity. (Wind and other alternatives lack sufficient scale and are discussed later.)

Alternatives for Generating Electricity

The first obstacle, therefore, is to replace the nuclear power plants currently in operation that are shut down, with new and improved nuclear power plants. (See Appendix H for a discussion of Generation III and IV nuclear reactor designs.)

The second obstacle is whether America has the political will to build new nuclear power plants. Twenty five new nuclear plants are on the drawing board with the first of these to be completed in 2015.

Many of these 25 plants are proposed for sites where there are existing nuclear power plants. While there will be opposition to building these plants, the fact that they will be next to existing plants favors their approval.

But what about nuclear power plants at new locations?

Will there be the political will to build Greenfield plants?

Powerful non-governmental organizations will probably fight the construction of any new nuclear power plant.

Here are quotations from some of these organizations:

From the Natural Resources Defense Council:

- New Nuclear Power Plants Are Not a Solution for America's Energy Needs.

From the Sierra Club:

- Nuclear Power: An Unsafe and Costly Choice.

From The National Wildlife Federation:

- There is a wide range of safer, cheaper, and faster ways to reduce global warming pollution other than expanding nuclear power.

Alternatives for Generating Electricity

From The Rocky Mountain Institute:

- Nuclear power plants are not only expensive, they're also financially extremely risky — nuclear power isn't a good way to curb climate change — nuclear power poses significant problems of radioactive waste disposal and the proliferation of potential nuclear weapons material.

These groups have powerful constituencies and make any revival of nuclear power problematic.

Coal

The words *Clean Coal* and *sequestration* are on the lips of every person involved in the coal industry. They have great public relations value, even though environmentalists say *Clean Coal* is an oxymoron.

The reality is that neither of these technologies are in place today; except for trial applications.

Clean Coal refers to a process where coal is cooked with steam and hot pressurized air to form gasses. CO_2 is then separated from the gasses, and the remaining gasses, primarily methane and hydrogen, are burned in a gas turbine that drives a generator to generate electricity. The unused heat leaving the gas turbine is used to generate steam in a boiler which then drives a steam turbine that drives a generator to generate electricity.

These plants are known as Integrated Gasification Combined Cycle (IGCC) plants.

IGCC plants can be built to capture CO_2, or not. None have yet been built carbon capture ready.

Future Gen, a research project, was scheduled for completion in 2014. It was to be the first IGCC plant built capable of carbon capture. Future Gen was cancelled by the Department of Energy due to the project's high costs; however, it may be revived if sufficient funds become available.

Only two IGCC commercial demonstration plants have been built in the United States. The Polk Power Station, 250 MW plant at Tampa Electric and the Wabash River Coal gasification and recovery project 262 MW unit.

Neither is carbon capture ready.

IGCC plants must be able to capture carbon if they are to reduce CO_2 emissions.

IGCC plants require a larger investment than a conventional pulverized coal power plant and the electricity generated by these plants will be more expensive. When carbon capture is included, the cost of electricity from an IGCC plant can be approximately twice the cost of electricity from a modern pulverized coal plant.

The purpose of IGCC plants is to capture CO_2 before the combustion process, but if there is no place to put the CO_2 the process is futile. This is where sequestration enters the picture.

The theory behind sequestration is that CO_2 can be liquefied and then pumped into underground storage where it will remain and not reenter the atmosphere.

While CO_2 may be captured from new IGCC power plants, assuming they work as proposed, how do we capture CO_2 from existing coal fired power plants?

Assuming existing plants can be modified, which will not always be possible due to space limitations, the issue becomes which process to use. Thus far, only field prototypes exist of the most promising processes for capturing CO_2 from existing coal fired power plants.

These processes either prepare the CO_2 in the flue gas for carbon capture, or target pre-combustion for combustion capture.

Alternatives for Generating Electricity

Amines are the most popular solvents for post combustion capture. Pre-combustion capture may involve other solvents. An oxy-combustion approach burns the coal in pure oxygen, making it easier to capture the CO_2. Other less well developed processes are also being explored.

Importantly, carbon capture processes will require de-rating existing coal fired power plants by 20 to 40%. Essentially, one new power plant will have to be built to replace the electricity no longer being generated when three power plants are retrofitted for carbon capture. Some units can be completely rebuilt with little loss of output, but this is analogous to building a new IGCC plant.[32]

While it probably will be possible to build new IGCC power plants capable of capturing CO_2, there is no proven technology for separating CO_2 from existing coal fired power plants.

See Exhibit II: Consequences of De-rating Coal Fired Power Plants.

Sequestration

Assuming it will be possible to retrofit all existing coal fired power plants to achieve carbon capture, and that all new coal fired power plants will be of the IGCC variety that allows for carbon capture, the CO_2 will have to be stored either underground or in the ocean.

Storing the CO_2 in the ocean is highly questionable since there is a strong probability the CO_2 will leak into the atmosphere. Some are now raising the specter of ocean acidification from CO_2 so sequestration in the ocean would appear to be out of the question.

Currently the largest underground sequestration operation is the Sleipner gas field where one million metric tons of CO_2 are injected annually into a saline aquifer under the North Sea.

For comparison purposes, the U. S. currently produces about 1,900 million metric tons of CO_2 each year from coal fired power plants.

EXHIBIT II

Consequences of De-rating Coal Fired Power Plants.

Retrofitting existing coal fired power plants will result in a loss of generating capacity of between 20% and 40%. The results can be viewed two ways.

1. **Cost of building replacement power plants**

   Existing installed capacity = 335,830,000 kW

   1/3 loss of capacity from de-rating = 110,824,000 kW

   Cost per kW to build a replacement plant = $2,800 per kW

   Investment to replace lost power = $310 billion

2. **Number of power plants to replace lost power**

   Number of existing coal fired power plants rated 100 MW and above = 417

   Number of coal plants that must be replaced = 138

Note that the cost of replacing power plants is nearly half the cost of the $700 billion financial bailout passed by Congress in October 2008. The cost of replacing power plants doesn't include the cost of sequestering the CO_2 from all coal fired power plants.

Sources:

Generating capacity from EIA report *Existing Capacity by Energy Source*, October 2007.

Number of units over 100 MW from Platts. EIA indicates there are additional 200 coal fired plants rated less than 100 MW, so number of replacement units could be greater.

Cost of new carbon capture ready coal fired power plant from McKinsey & Company report, *Reducing U.S. Greenhouse Gas Emissions: How Much at What Cost?,* December 2007. Cost excludes financing costs.

Alternatives for Generating Electricity

While federal and state governments are currently inventorying geologic formations, regulatory bodies will need to be established to ensure that the sequestered CO_2 doesn't escape into the atmosphere or into adjoining geologic formations where it might cause harm.

Many geologic formations, especially where oil and gas drilling took place, have abandoned wells or openings whose locations are not known. Each geologic formation will have to be surveyed to identify these and other possible escape routes for CO_2.

The issue of ownership of geologic formations has not yet been addressed.

Who owns the geologic formations into which the CO_2 is to be injected?

Sorting ownership issues could take decades, or require government intervention through "takings" by eminent domain ... if eminent domain is even applicable.

Another unresolved issue involves legal liability if CO_2 escapes or causes harm.

Finally there is the issue of how to transport the liquid CO_2 from the coal fired power plant to the appropriate geologic formation.

Transporting all the captured CO_2 to an appropriate geologic formation is an immense task.

Each cubic meter of coal when burned completely, produces six cubic meters of liquefied CO_2.

If two thirds of all CO_2 emissions from coal fired power plants were captured and compressed to a liquid, its volume would equal America's consumption of 20 million barrels of oil per day.[33]

Sequestration will require building thousands of miles of new pipelines.

Alternatives for Generating Electricity

Building new pipelines will not be an easy task. Proponents of sequestration have pointed to pipelines built by oil companies for CO2 injection to stimulate oil well production to demonstrate the feasibility of building pipelines.

There are approximately 3,000 miles of existing CO2 pipelines built for supplying CO2 for enhanced oil production.

Building a few pipelines in the sparsely populated West is different from building 24" or 40" diameter pipelines in densely populated Middle Western or Eastern states.

Will people want pipelines built in their back yard or neighborhood?

Permitting, land acquisition and rights of way, including "takings" by eminent domain, are not trivial issues.

A cursory look at the Carbon Sequestration Atlas of the U.S. and Canada, shows there are very few geologic formations for sequestering CO2 emissions east of the Appalachian mountains in the fourteen states from Maine to Florida.[34] One third of the electricity generated in the U.S. is generated in these fourteen states which means that most of the CO2 emissions from these power plants will have to be transported by pipelines to geologic formations in the Midwest.

There are at least 99 coal fired power plants east of the Appalachian Mountains that will use a system of pipelines extending from each power plant to geologic formations in the Midwest.[35]

The accompanying *CO2 Pipeline Map* shows where pipelines would be needed for transporting liquid CO2 from coal fired power plants to the nearest geologic formation where CO2 might be sequestered.

These findings are partially supported by the Pacific Northwest National Laboratory (PNNL) that issued its report, *Future CO$_2$ Pipeline Not as Onerous as Some Think,* January 2009. The report's title is misleading since the report concluded that 11,000 to 23,000 miles of pipelines will have to be built.

The *CO2 Pipeline Map* (See Figure I) was developed using the government's Carbon Sequestration Atlas together with the map from Platt's showing the location of 417 U.S. coal fired power plants rated 100 MW and above. (Some locations have more than one power plant.) Possible pipeline routes were mapped using this data, but no attempt was made to bypass cities, geographic barriers or environmental hazards.

These will be high pressure pipelines with pressures of around 2,000 psi. A 24 inch diameter pipeline, therefore, would have a wall thickness of approximately one inch.[36] The pipelines would be made of standard carbon steel assuming moisture is excluded from the liquid CO_2; otherwise stainless steel pipe would be needed to avoid corrosion.

Pipelines will require periodic compressor stations where incoming pressure might be 1700 psi and outgoing pressure may be 2100 psi.

There will only be limited opportunities to utilize rights of way of existing oil and natural gas pipelines. Most existing oil and natural gas pipelines east of the Mississippi travel in a northeasterly direction, while pipelines carrying CO_2 will need to run in a westerly or northwesterly direction.[37] The majority of CO_2 pipelines will lie east of the Mississippi.

Some coal fired power plants are located in urban areas such as Philadelphia, Washington DC and Chicago, where the pipelines will have to be laid underneath streets and through suburbs.

Obtaining rights of way from property owners will be a time consuming process and may require government to exercise eminent domain to take the property. When traversing residential areas it will almost certainly require condemnation of people's homes.

Alternatives for Generating Electricity

A right of way for a CO2 pipeline will be approximately 100 feet wide, 40 feet for the pipeline and an additional 60 feet that's required for pipeline construction.[38]

Takings are virtually certain due to their locations in well developed eastern states and their routes through established communities.

The political process involving public hearings and appeals to various Congressmen, including the potential for lawsuits, will likely make obtaining rights of way a political circus.

Construction, ownership and management of the pipelines will be an issue.

West of the Appalachian Mountains, companies whose power plants are located close to an appropriate geologic formation may choose to own the pipelines.

East of the Appalachian Mountains it's likely that major trunk lines will gather CO2 from multiple power plants, thereby reducing the number and overall length of pipelines. The trunk lines would be owned by corporations acting as "transport companies".

The "transport company" approach using trunk lines raises additional issues.

Presumably, ownership of the CO2 will be transferred from the power plant owner to the "transport company" when any feeder line intersects the trunk line. Leaks and liability issues will presumably lie with the owner of the pipeline carrying the CO2.

Quality standards will have to be established for the liquid CO2. Pressure and temperature will have to be rigidly controlled. The permissible level of contaminants, such as moisture, will have to be established and monitored. Excess moisture can result in the formation of Carbonic Acid. Limiting moisture content to below 30 lbs/million standard cubic feet is standard for the industry.

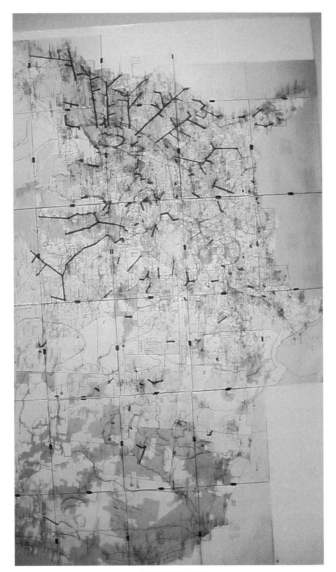

FIGURE I
U.S. CO2 Pipelines

Alternatives for Generating Electricity

Safety will be an issue.

CO_2 is heavier than air and odorless, so pipeline leaks have the potential of creating dangerous, possibly life threatening situations. As noted above, many miles of pipelines will traverse residential areas.

There is also the danger of violent expansion from a leak where pressure suddenly drops from 2,000 psi to 14.7 psi.

By comparing the location of coal fired power plants with the geologic formations pictured in the Carbon Sequestration Atlas of the U.S. and Canada, it's possible to estimate the number of miles of pipelines required to transport all the CO_2 emissions from the power plant to the nearest available geologic formation. (See Exhibit III and Appendix B.)

These estimates assume the geologic formations are actually suitable for storing CO_2 emissions without leaking to the atmosphere or to adjoining formations.

Collectively, these pipelines would be over thirteen times longer than the Trans Alaska Pipeline System (TAPS) which stretches 800 miles from Prudhoe Bay to Valdez.

The MIT study on the future of coal states: "In sum, the demonstration of an integrated coal conversion, CO_2 capture, and sequestration capability is an enormous system engineering and integration challenge."

It also says that reliable risk assessment of sequestration projects is lacking.

The mere fact that industry has organized a new Association dedicated to "resolving the panoply of issues arising from" carbon sequestration, demonstrates that there are many unanswered questions surrounding sequestration.[39]

EXHIBIT III

Estimated length of Pipelines
from
Coal Fired Power Plants 100 MW and greater:

Connecting 99 Coal Plants Located East of Appalachian Mountains to Midwest Oil & Gas Reservoirs = 5,006 miles

Connecting 177 Midwest Coal Plants to Midwest Geologic Formations = 3,502 miles

Connecting 141 Remaining Coal Plants in U.S. to Nearest Geologic Formations = 2,305 miles

TOTAL REQUIRED MILES = 10,813 miles

These estimates are based on a logical grouping of coal fired power plants connected to hypothetical pipelines to transport liquid CO_2 to the nearest geologic formation.

The total required miles probably represents the minimum requirement, as there is great likelihood that some of the formations will not be suitable for storing CO_2.

Platts reports there are 417 coal fired power plants rated 100 MW and above, these represent 97% of total installed capacity. The EIA indicates there are additional coal fired units rated less than 100 MW, and these will also require additional miles of pipeline or be shut down.

See Appendix B for details.

Alternatives for Generating Electricity

Natural Gas

Natural gas power plants produce about 45% less CO_2 per kWhr than do traditional coal fired plants. This is one reason why, in recent years, natural gas plants have been built rather than coal fired plants.

Many communities are also prohibiting the construction of coal fired plants leaving newly developed large (480MW Combined Cycle) natural gas power plants as the only non-nuclear alternative for providing base load power.

Organizations such as the Sierra Club are lobbying communities to not invest in or build new coal fired power plants.[40]

Several organizations have been tracking the number of planned coal fired power plants that have been cancelled because of concerns about global warming. Earth2tech.com has published a map showing 15 cancelled plants, not counting the eight that TXU had originally planned for Texas.

An example of the reasoning behind these cancellations is the statement by the Director of Kansas Department of Health and Environment who said it would be "irresponsible to ignore global warming concerns" when he denied a permit for the Sunflower Electric Power Corporation plants.

Replacing all existing coal fired plants with natural gas will not achieve an 80% reduction in CO_2 emissions for the electric sector.

The price of natural gas doubled between 2000 and 2005, which cost American jobs. Natural gas prices were forecast to remain at these high levels for several years in the future.[41]

Higher prices for natural gas used as feedstock by the chemical industry have already caused a loss of jobs.

By one count, 90,000 American jobs have been lost since 2000 due to the shortage and resulting high price of natural gas. The Nitrogen fertilizer industry has shut down 36% of its operations since 2000 due to the high price of natural gas.[42]

63

Alternatives for Generating Electricity

New drilling techniques have resulted in an oversupply of natural gas so the price has recently come down. This is good news for homeowners since natural gas is the primary method for heating homes.

There is still the problem of obtaining leases and drilling permits, especially on Federal lands where the Bureau of Land Management has control over leases. Proposals to use natural gas in automobiles could change the supply situation.

Hydro

Conventional hydro power, as differentiated from pumped storage, emits no CO_2. (Some environmental groups oppose this assertion and say that reservoirs created by dams can emit CO_2.)

Currently, Hydro accounts for 7% of total electricity generation. Every indication is that the amount of electricity generated from Hydro will decline rather than increase.

Environmental groups are insisting that dams be dismantled, either to protect salmon or to restore scenic vistas and historic sites. Four dams on the Snake River are being targeted for removal because they interfere with salmon.

Groups fight against building new dams so as to protect the ecology.

In April 2007, the California Senate rejected a proposal to build two new hydro-electric dams.

It is doubtful that new dams will be built and it is very likely that dams, especially smaller ones, will be dismantled.

Hydrokinetic units have recently been developed and may be able to produce electricity for the grid; however, the amount generated will be relatively small.

Alternatives for Generating Electricity

In-stream Hydrokinetic generators are small units, using propellers or water turbines connected to a generator, to generate electricity.

Water flowing through the turbine causes the turbine to rotate. It is an experimental concept that has yet to be proven on any large scale. The amount of electricity each unit will actually produce when water flow speeds vary is unknown. Electrical equipment installed underwater also incurs higher maintenance costs.

These small units, three to twelve feet in diameter, which generate small amounts of electricity, and require water flowing at least five feet per second, would be placed in rivers with their output connected to the grid. Whether large numbers of these units can be placed in rivers without interfering with shipping or causing environmental problems has yet to be determined.

There is no publicly available data to indicate the cost, in $ per kWh to the consumer.

The units are rated 100 kW and lower. Two experimental, 12 foot diameter units, rated 100 kW, are being installed at a unique location behind an existing dam, in the Mississippi River at Hastings, Minnesota. They are being located in the clean discharge flow of existing hydro units where water speeds are reasonably constant and the debris has been eliminated. In most situations, hydrokinetic units located in rivers would likely be exposed to debris and variable water flows and have a capacity factor closer to 30% than the units being located in Hastings. Depending on the eventually determined capacity factor, it would require installing hundreds of thousands of these units in America's rivers to have an appreciable impact on the availability of electricity.

With virtually no units currently installed, it is impossible to determine whether hydrokinetic generators will function as intended or whether they will create environmental or other dangers.

Alternatives for Generating Electricity

Wind

Wind power is being touted as a way to generate electricity without producing CO_2.

But, can wind power replace existing coal fired plants or be a substitute for new coal fired plants?

Coal fired and nuclear power plants are base load plants. They typically are around 600 to 1,000 MW in size and produce large amounts of electricity on a steady basis. This is in contrast to natural gas power plants that generally provide peaking power.[43] (Peaks in usage of electricity occur when there are large air conditioning loads or at certain times of the day, such as in the evening when cooking and lighting loads coincide.)

Wind turbines cannot be used for base loads because they provide electricity intermittently. If the wind doesn't blow, wind turbines can't generate electricity. Or, if the wind blows too hard the wind turbines must be shut down. Wind is unreliable.

A wind turbine rated 1.5 MW (typical size of today's units) is actually a .5 MW unit after considering its capacity factor.[44] (The wind blows 30% of the time at speeds that can generate electricity, so units only produce 30% of the rated nameplate.)[45]

This means it requires 2,000 wind turbines to replace one 1,000 MW coal fired or nuclear power plant. The largest number of wind turbines installed in any single year in the United States was approximately 4900 units in 2008.[46]

See Exhibit IV: Comparing Wind Turbines and Nuclear Energy.

Wind supplied a minuscule amount of electricity in the U.S. in 2006. (See Table IV)

Alternatives for Generating Electricity

EXHIBIT IV

Comparing Wind Turbines and Nuclear Energy.

Current wind turbine production models Rated 1.5 MW
- ✓ With 30% capacity factor produces
3.9 million kWh/year

A 1,000 MW Nuclear Power Plant
- ✓ With 90% capacity factor produces
7,880 million kWh/year

Capacity factor compares the actual output of a wind turbine with its rated name plate.

The amount of electricity produced by a wind turbine varies with wind speed and density so there are differing outputs over a range of wind speeds during the day while the wind turbine is in operation.

A wind turbine begins generating electricity when the wind reaches a speed of around 6 miles per hour, reaches rated capacity with wind speeds of around 31 miles per hour, and is cut out and prevented from generating electricity at wind speeds in excess of around 56 miles per hour.

An example of the variations encountered when determining capacity factor is that output from a wind turbine varies depending on air temperature. This means that the wind turbine will have lower output on a hot, sunny day just when air conditioning loads are increasing.

Electricity generated by wind turbines is inherently intermittent, volatile and, from the point of view of being available for dispatch on the grid, unreliable.

These are some of the reasons why wind cannot replace coal or nuclear power.

Alternatives for Generating Electricity

Wind turbine manufacturers were at capacity in 2008 and would be hard pressed to produce enough wind turbines to replace more than a few coal fired or nuclear power plants, let alone several hundred.

Wind turbines are also coming under attack from several quarters, including environmentalists. Wind turbines kill birds and bats and interfere with historically valuable scenic vistas. Wind turbines are also an expensive way to generate electricity.[47]

Maintenance costs for wind turbines are now being more closely scrutinized. Gear boxes have been failing within five years and blades have also been failing. Suzlon, an Indian manufacturer with a worldwide market share of 9%, is planning on replacing 1,251 blades in the United States.[48] An eleven year old wind turbine buckled and collapsed in New Hampshire, dumping its 28 ton nacelle into a field. Other catastrophic failures have occurred in Idaho, Minnesota, New York and Pennsylvania.[49]

Wind turbines are supposed to last for twenty years.

Geothermal

Geothermal power plants produced substantially less than 1% of the electricity used in the United States in 2006. U.S. geothermal generation capacity is currently around 3,000 MW and could be increased to around 5,000 MW by 2020.

There are futuristic geothermal proposals but these have little chance of becoming significant producers of electricity in the foreseeable future. The Google energy plan refers to "hot dry rocks" as "enhanced geothermal systems" (EGS) and claims that 65 gigawatts of electricity can be derived from this source. Australia has pioneered in this effort, drilling its first 14,000 foot well in 2003. Thus far, "hot dry rocks" is still experimental. (See Appendix C for information on geothermal generation of electricity including "hot dry rocks".)

Alternatives for Generating Electricity

Other Renewables

Table III shows the amount of electricity generated by renewable sources (other than Hydro).

It is doubtful that any of these sources can be substantially increased. Additionally, some of these renewable sources, such as wood, produce GHG.

While recent laboratory advances in solar film may make solar more attractive, solar is bound to remain a niche player for the foreseeable future.

Other solar technologies, such as concentrating technologies, could potentially generate substantial amounts of electricity. They would be limited to the Southwestern U.S. due to available sunlight. Theoretically a 100 MW solar power tower could be built on 1,000 acres of vacant land in the southwest to generate electricity during the day time. A few parabolic trough systems have been built, but these other solar technologies are still largely experimental.

A major problem with solar is that it only generates electricity when the sun shines. Practical systems do not yet exist where solar can be used for generating electricity at night. While it might be possible to build huge solar installations in the Southwest,[50] solar's inability to generate electricity at night precludes counting on solar as a substitute for coal or nuclear power generation.

No one mentions that these immense solar panels must be cleaned, otherwise electric output declines.

Developing a breakthrough technology for storing electricity could change this equation, though transmitting electricity to the East Coast and Midwest would still be a challenge.

While solar is intriguing and has great potential, it is not ready for prime time. Cap & trade regulations cannot count on solar as a proven technology ready to replace conventional power generation.

(See Appendix D for discussion of solar power.)

Alternatives for Generating Electricity

Experimental methods for generating electricity include wave power and tidal action. A few such installations have been built to determine the feasibility of using the motion of water to drive either turbines or pumps to generate electricity. These units could be installed in rivers, along coast lines and in areas where there is tidal motion. It's doubtful these experimental methods could supply a significant amount of electricity in the foreseeable future.

Conclusion: Alternatives for electricity.

It is not possible with today's technologies (other than nuclear) to reduce CO_2 emissions by 80% from the generation of electricity without decreasing the supply of electricity and thereby causing blackouts, factory closings and unemployment.

Since the generation of electricity accounts for 39% of all U.S. CO_2 emissions, it is unreasonable to expect that other sectors can reduce their emissions by substantially greater than 80% to make up for any short fall in the electric sector.

The reasons why it's appropriate to say an 80% reduction is not possible with today's technologies (without decreasing the supply of electricity) include:

- Nuclear power plants could decrease in number by 2050 as their operating licenses expire.

- IGCC *Clean-Coal* power plants are still under development. Only two developmental plants have been built and neither is carbon capture ready.

- Wind cannot substitute for coal fired or nuclear power plants. Wind is intermittent and unreliable.

- Other renewables such as solar are too limited as to where they may be installed and are too small in scale to substitute for coal fired or nuclear power plants.

70

Alternatives for Generating Electricity

- Sequestration is still only a concept that needs to overcome at least four hurdles.

  1. Capturing CO_2 in existing coal fired power plants as well as in new IGCC plants.

  2. Building thousands of miles of pipelines to transport liquid CO_2.

  3. Identifying underground geologic formations that won't leak.

  4. Resolving ownership and legal issues.

- The population is forecast to increase by 139 million new Americans by 2050.

With nuclear plants having to be decommissioned when their operating licenses expire and with 139 million additional Americans wanting air conditioning and lighting, new coal fired plants will have to be built if Americans are to have the electricity they need. These coal fired plants will probably be modern, super-critical pulverized coal plants.

But, if people in government prevent the construction of new coal fired power plants so as to reduce CO_2 emissions, there will be a shortage of electricity.

Alternatives for Generating Electricity

U.S. Sector/Source	2007	
	Thousand kWh	% Total
Biomass	55,400,235	**1.33%**
Waste	16,884,973	0.41%
Landfill Gas	6,199,777	0.15%
MSW[a] Biogenic	8,567,940	0.21%
Other Biomass	2,117,257	0.05%
Wood & Derived Fuels	38,515,262	0.93%
Geothermal	14,838,636	**0.36%**
Solar/ PV	606,082	**0.01%**
Wind	32,143,244	**0.77%**
Total U.S. Net Generation	4,156,745,000	**100%**

Table III

Data from U. S. Energy Information Agency

a= Municipal Solid Waste

Chapter 9

Gasoline Alternatives

Gasoline usage accounted for 20% of U.S. CO2 emissions in 2004. Virtually all of this gasoline was used for cars and light trucks (SUV's).

There were 223 million cars and light trucks on the road in the U.S. in 2003.

Primarily because of an increase in population, the number of cars and light trucks forecast to be on the road in 2050 is 321 million.

Once again, the increase in population will make it increasingly difficult to reduce CO2 emissions from gasoline by 80%.

Another factor that will make it difficult to achieve any major near term reductions in gasoline usage is that cars and light trucks have an average lifespan of 15 years. Cars and SUV's sold today will be on the road using gasoline in the mid 2020's.

Ethanol

Ethanol is considered to have zero CO2 emissions as it is assumed the corn used to make ethanol will absorb as much CO2 from the atmosphere as it emits when burned in a vehicle.

Ethanol could be one way to reduce CO2 emissions from vehicles, though new studies have shown that more CO2 is emitted than is saved when land is converted to grow corn.[51]

Currently, U.S. ethanol is produced from corn. There is serious concern about using corn to make ethanol. Corn is a basic food crop and is used as feed to produce beef.[52] Using corn for ethanol could drive up the cost of food (which it already has done in Mexico with higher prices for tortillas).

Research is being conducted on how to make ethanol from cellulose. If cellulosic ethanol becomes viable it will allow making

Gasoline Alternatives

ethanol from corn stover (i.e., corn stalks) or switchgrass or other fast growing grasses or trees.

There currently are 30 million acres of unused U.S. farm land enrolled in the Conservation Reserve.[53] If all 30 million acres were added to the acreage currently used to grow corn used for making ethanol, a total of around 1.3 million barrels per day of ethanol could be produced in the U.S. This represents around 10% of daily gasoline usage in the U.S.

Theoretically total production could be doubled if corn stalks could be used for making cellulosic ethanol.

Under the most favorable conditions, it might be possible to reduce gasoline usage by around 20% by using both ethanol from corn and cellulosic ethanol.

This would represent a corresponding 20% reduction in CO_2 emissions from gasoline; a far cry from 80%.

Electric Vehicles

Electric vehicles, probably in the form of Plug-in Hybrid Electric Vehicles (PHEV'S), have the potential for achieving significant reductions in gasoline usage and a possible corresponding reduction in CO_2 emissions.

Prototype PHEV's built by interested groups have demonstrated the PHEV's ability to get over 100 miles per gallon of gasoline. They achieve this performance by operating much of the time on battery power.

The PHEV would only use the gasoline engine when it was driven at higher speeds. Since most cars are driven only 35 miles each day for commuting, these cars will not require very much gasoline. The batteries will be recharged nightly from a 120 volt outlet. In essence, every garage becomes a battery charging station.

74

Gasoline Alternatives

Estimates indicate that up to 75% of drivers have access to an outlet for recharging batteries.[54]

PHEV's depend on improved battery technology. Currently the most promising new battery technology is the Lithium-ion battery.

Li-ion batteries come with different chemistries.

Most Li-ion batteries using cobalt have a tendency to experience runaway temperatures with resulting fires.

Other Li-ion chemistries use manganese and phosphate, but these had their capacity drop by 80% when tested over seven years.[55]

Another major problem with batteries is their short shelf life or ability to sustain charging over a long period of time or from multiple charges. Charging and shelf life problems do not usually affect products such as cell phones or lap top computers. But they do affect an application where the battery must last for 100,000 miles and withstand thousands of charges.

A123Systems Corporation is developing a Li-ion battery using nanophosphate battery chemistry. This nano technology was developed at MIT and its developers help found A123Systems Corporation. It has received over $100 million in venture capital funding.

The A123Systems Li-ion batteries have been used by Black and Decker in their hand tools. Over 10 million of these batteries have been made annually for Black and Decker and other companies.

A123Systems appeared to have demonstrated its ability to ramp up manufacturing of Li-ion batteries.[56] Their next challenge will be to demonstrate that their batteries can be used in PHEV's with satisfactory lifetime performance.

GM, however, selected LG Chem Ltd. of Korea as supplier of the battery for its *Volt* automobile because LG Chem had larger production capacity and a longer track record.

Gasoline Alternatives

GM has announced it will produce the *Volt* in 2010. This could be the first year a mass produced PHEV will be available for the average consumer.[57]

Many other manufacturers have recently announced plans for producing PHEV's.

There are two versions of plug-in electric vehicles being developed today. The first, or series version, runs for forty miles on battery and then a small internal combustion engine kicks in to maintain the battery's charge so the car can continue to run in the electric mode. GM's volt typifies this version.

The second, or parallel type, runs on battery power for forty miles and then a full size internal combustion engine takes over to power the car on gasoline.

The modified Prius best typifies this version.

Both versions can recharge the battery from an outlet in the garage.

If 7,000 PHEV's are sold in 2010 and the number sold increase by 30% every year thereafter, it won't be until the mid 2050's before 75% of the cars on the road are PHEV's. Since PHEV's can use ethanol in their internal combustion engine it can be assumed that only the remaining 25% (61 million vehicles) will use gasoline.[58]

This is clearly a very ambitious forecast. It assumes a 30% annual increase in PHEV's sold which is highly unlikely for two reasons:

1. PHEV's will likely cost up to $10,000 more than conventional cars due primarily to the higher cost of the Li-ion battery; even with a tax credit.

2. Given a choice, some consumers will prefer the handling of traditional gasoline driven vehicles.

DOE predicts sales of PHEV's in 2030 to be only 2400 vehicles.[59]

Gasoline Alternatives

There is a possibility that existing Hybrid vehicles can be retrofitted with a Li-ion battery. This would slightly increase the number of PHEV's on the road.

A123Systems has indicated they are selling a retrofit battery package.

The think tank, TSAugust (publishers of *Carbon Folly*), suggested that Li-ion batteries be leased; where the monthly lease cost would be offset by the savings in gasoline usage. A leasing program such as this would require a huge capital investment, but if both the car manufacturers and electric utilities leased the batteries such a program would be feasible.

It is in the self interest of electric utilities to lease batteries. Batteries in the PHEV's will be recharged from people's homes during off peak hours. This represents a business opportunity for electric utilities where they will be selling electricity from generators that would otherwise be idle. Their costs will be variable costs as the capital investment in generation and transmission equipment will already have been made.

While PHEV's can result in reduced CO_2 emissions from gasoline, the electric utility will emit CO_2 as it produces electricity for recharging the batteries.

A study by the Pacific Northwest National Laboratory[60] determined that 43% of the existing cars and light trucks could be PHEV's before new generation and transmission infrastructure would be required. Because the number of vehicles will increase due to population growth, this percentage would decrease to around 30% in the mid 2050's when 75%[61] of vehicles would be PHEV's (under the previous optimistic assumptions).

In other words, new generating capacity will be required at some point in the future. Given today's available technology, these new power generation plants will probably be coal fired.

Gasoline Alternatives

More importantly, the issue is: How much additional CO_2 will be produced from generating the electricity required to recharge PHEV Li-ion batteries that displace the use of gasoline?

This depends on what energy source is used to generate the needed electricity. A combination of coal fired and natural gas is the most likely source.

A rough calculation shows that if 75% of the vehicles on the road in 2050 are PHEV's, CO_2 emissions will be approximately 959 MMT (540 from generating the required electricity plus 418 from the 25% of gasoline powered cars remaining on the road) compared with 1162.6 MMT from gasoline alone in 2004. (See Appendix E for Calculation.)

While these calculations are admittedly rough, an optimistic scenario would have PHEV's reducing CO_2 emissions 18% by 2050. (More if nuclear power is used to generate the required additional electricity.)

Converting 75% of all cars and light trucks (SUV's) to PHEV's by 2050 will still result in CO_2 emissions of 959 MMT which far exceeds 191 MMT. (CO_2 emissions of 191 MMT from gasoline would be allowed under the proposed legislation requiring an 80% reduction in CO_2 emissions.)

It should be noted that PHEV's can also reduce America's dependence on foreign oil by a much larger percentage.

Natural Gas

Oil tycoon Pickens has proposed using natural gas to power America's automobiles. The purpose of his proposal is to reduce America's dependence on foreign oil. It would, however, also reduce CO_2 emissions.

Four issues affect whether natural gas could be used to replace gasoline in an effort to reduce CO_2 emissions.

Gasoline Alternatives

1. Is there sufficient natural gas available in the United States to supply most of the automobiles in the United States?
2. Are there sufficient fueling stations?
3. Can manufacturers readily convert to producing vehicles using compressed natural gas (CNG)?
4. Would natural gas reduce CO_2 emissions by 80%?

See Exhibit V: Replacing Gasoline with Natural Gas

Exhibit V shows that the United States has an ample supply of natural gas and that automobile manufacturers could easily reintroduce CNG vehicles.

An overriding problem is that there are too few fueling stations and that it would cost a substantial amount of money to establish enough fueling stations to accommodate widespread usage of CNG vehicles. The option of home fueling is not overly attractive because of its high cost and the time required to refuel a CNG vehicle.

Even if every vehicle in the United States used CNG it would reduce CO_2 emissions by only around 30% which is not nearly enough to meet the 80% reduction required by proposed cap & trade legislation.[62]

Hydrogen Powered Vehicles

An alternative to electric vehicles that has received considerable attention is the use of hydrogen to fuel the vehicles.[63]

The three most significant reasons why hydrogen vehicles are not likely to become available in the near future are:

- The problem of storing hydrogen on the vehicle
- The cost of fuel cells
- The problems associated with producing and distributing hydrogen

79

EXHIBIT V

Replacing Gasoline with Natural Gas

NG Availability

U.S. 2007 Production[a] = 19.3 trillion cubic feet (tcf)

✓ New AK Pipeline 2015 adds 1.6 tcf

Proved & undiscovered reserves = 415 tcf

Amount required to replace 100% of Vehicles = 15.7 tcf

NG Vehicle Availability

Factory Built:

✓ Currently only Civic GS

✓ GM, Ford Discontinued Production

❖ CNG & Bi-Fuel Vehicles Made in Europe

Retrofitting

✓ Limited potential. Few kits & very expensive

Fueling Availability

Currently approximately 800 public fueling stations

✓ Cost $1 million for each new station
✓ Need minimum 20,000 fueling stations[b]

Home fueling

✓ Fuel Maker cost $11,000 for ten hour refill

Sources: a: Energy Information Administration
   b: Navigant Consulting Inc.

Gasoline Alternatives

Hydrogen Storage

Compressed hydrogen has been stored on demonstration cars in cylinders at 10,000 psi and at 5,000 psi. These cylinders require considerable space on a vehicle and it is extremely difficult to design a vehicle around these cylinders. While these cylinders are probably safe, there is some concern about the high pressure and what might happen in an accident.

Hydrogen has also been stored in demonstration vehicles in liquid form. This requires cooling hydrogen to -423 degrees F and then storing it in, what is essentially a thermos bottle, on the vehicle. This method of storage raises similar concerns as storage in high pressure cylinders.

Research is underway to find a metal hydride that can absorb hydrogen and quickly release it on demand. Until now no such material has been discovered or developed.

Fuel Cells

"Fuel cells of various types have been under development for many years and have been used successfully in the space program and in stationary power generation. Commercial fuel cells are on the market today for power generation, either as backup power, remote stand alone power plants or cogeneration."

Proton Exchange Membrane (PEM) Fuel Cells that operate at relatively low temperatures seem to be the type receiving the most attention at this time for possible use in vehicles and in residential applications.

Fuel cells are extremely expensive. By one account they are ten times more expensive than internal combustion engines.

Honda recently made headlines when it leased a limited number of its FCX Clarity hydrogen fuel cell vehicles in California. Other companies have also leased a limited number of fuel cell vehicles.

These test vehicles are not for sale.

Gasoline Alternatives

Hydrogen Production and Distribution

Hydrogen can be produced using electrolysis, from methane gas and in high temperature nuclear reactors.

It requires 1 kg (2.2 pounds) of hydrogen to displace one gallon of gasoline. Calculations show that using hydrogen in an internal combustion engine (ICE) to replace all the gasoline used today will require an amount of electricity roughly equal to all the electricity currently produced in the U.S. Since fuel cells are about twice as efficient as ICE's, the amount of electricity would be cut in half.

The end result for fuel cells is that about as much CO_2 will be emitted from generating the required electricity for electrolysis as is produced from using gasoline, unless nuclear is used to generate the electricity.

Hydrogen could be produced from methane and could be a byproduct of *Clean-Coal* power plants. Producing hydrogen from natural gas (methane) would be less efficient than using it directly in CNG vehicles.

Electrolysis is the most practical method for producing hydrogen in a distributed system. (It can also be produced locally using natural gas.)

Producing hydrogen from methane (possibly from IGCC power plants) or in nuclear reactors would be done at central locations. Hydrogen produced at central locations will have to be trucked in liquid form (with an energy loss from liquefying the gas) to distributed fueling stations. Alternatively, a new system of special pipelines could be built. (Natural gas pipelines are not suitable for hydrogen as the hydrogen will attack the pipes.)

* * *

Gasoline Alternatives

Conclusion: Alternatives for Gasoline.

Short of gasoline rationing or prohibiting people from owning automobiles, it is not feasible to reduce CO_2 emissions from gasoline 80% by 2050.

Ethanol can not by itself, under the most favorable of scenarios, reduce CO_2 emissions by anywhere near 80%.

Electric vehicles may be able to reduce CO_2 emissions by about 18%, but not until 2050. The savings from gasoline emissions are partially offset by CO_2 emissions from additional generation of electricity (unless the electricity is generated using nuclear power).

Vehicles using compressed natural gas can reduce CO_2 emissions by only around 30%.

Hydrogen powered vehicles are not likely to become feasible for decades, and similar to electric vehicles, cannot reduce CO_2 emissions significantly; certainly not anywhere near 80%. Producing hydrogen by electrolysis, probably the most logical approach to hydrogen production and distribution could result in a net increase in CO_2 emissions due to the additional generation of electricity.

Rationing gasoline, the only viable way to cut CO_2 emissions by 80%, would have a devastating effect on the economy. If nothing else does, rationing will kill the automobile industry.

Chapter 10

Alternatives Available for Other Sectors

Industrial Sector

CO_2 emissions from the Industrial Sector amounted to 1,069.3 MMT in 2004. Industry accounts for 18% of total U.S. CO_2 emissions.

Industrial companies typically make investment decisions based on return on investment. For this reason industry is already fairly efficient in the way it utilizes resources. This makes achieving further reductions in CO_2 emissions more difficult.

For example, most manufacturing plants and offices already use fluorescent and high intensity discharge (HID) lighting so there are limited opportunities to reduce electric consumption for lighting. (CO_2 from electricity is part of the Electric Sector and is not included as part of the 1,069.3 MMT emissions attributed to the Industrial Sector)

Table IV shows the CO_2 emissions by industry segment.

Table V shows emissions by source for these industry segments. Both natural gas and oil are used as feedstocks for products in addition to being fuel sources. (For example, natural gas is used to make fertilizers and other chemical products.)

DuPont has demonstrated it is possible to reduce CO_2 emissions. There likely are incremental opportunities across all industries.

Natural gas is also used in manufacturing processes. Natural gas fired ovens are used to dry paint, harden tools, bake transformer coils, heat-treat metals, plus a myriad of other operations.

As mentioned above, industry generally installs the most efficient equipment so it is not a simple matter to reduce natural gas usage in these types of processes. (Electricity can be used in some applications to substitute for natural gas, but this results in CO_2 emissions from generating electricity.)

85

U.S. Industrial CO2 Emissions 2002		
Industry	MMT	% Total
Petroleum	280.2	33%
Chemicals	211.6	25%
Metals	119.0	14%
Paper	60.0	7%
Minerals	64.3	7%
Other Manufacturing	125.3	15%
Total	860.4	100%

Table IV

Latest available data by Industry type.

Source: *Emission of Greenhouse Gasses in the United States 2005* by DOE Energy Information Administration.

MMT = Million Metric Tons

Coal is largely used to produce coke which is used in the steel industry.

The U.S. economy has been shifting from energy intensive industries to service industries such as finance that are less energy intensive. Until now, energy intensive industries have been inclined to move off shore largely for cost reasons.

U.S. Industrial CO2 Emissions 2004

Source	MMT	% Total
Natural Gas	441.9	41%
Oil	440.6	41%
Coal	181.0	17%
Miscellaneous	5.8	1%
Total	1069.3	100%

Table V

Source: *Emission of Greenhouse Gasses in the United States 2005* by DOE Energy Information Administration.

MMT = Million Metric Tons

Conclusion: Industrial Sector

Small reductions in CO2 are possible in the Industrial Sector, but it is not possible to achieve an 80% reduction unless energy intensive industries move offshore, *along with their jobs*.

* * *

Transportation Sector (Excluding Gasoline)

Transportation, excluding gasoline, produces 771.1 MMT of CO2 emissions, or 13% of total U.S. CO2 emissions.

The bulk of these CO2 emissions come from two sources:

- Distillates (Diesel Fuel), 56%
- Jet Fuel, 31%

Alternatives Available for Other Sectors

Diesel fuel is used mostly by heavy duty trucks and railroads. Off highway vehicles and marine applications (e.g., barges) also use significant quantities of diesel fuel.

Trucks, railroads and barges transport virtually all of America's goods. Diesel engines have been in existence for over 100 years so improvements in CO_2 emissions will be modest.

Jet engines have been substantially improved over the years. One measure of this is passenger miles traveled compared with CO_2 emissions from jet fuel. Since 1990 passenger miles traveled have increased by 55% while jet fuel CO_2 emissions have increased by only 8%.

While continued improvements in jet engines can hold the rate of increase in CO_2 emissions down, they can't reduce CO_2 emissions unless air travel is discouraged and fewer people travel by air.

Conclusion: Transportation Sector

It will be extremely difficult to reduce CO_2 emissions from the Transportation Sector (excluding gasoline) by 80% without reducing the amount of goods transported by trucks, railroads and barges or by curtailing air travel.

As long as the economy continues to grow, CO_2 emissions from the Transportation Sector are likely to grow; perhaps at a slower rate with improved diesel fuel and jet engines.

The 139 million additional Americans by 2050 will demand more goods as well as access to air travel.

* * *

Alternatives Available for Other Sectors

Residential Sector

The residential sector produced 374.7 MMT of CO_2 emissions in 2004, which was 6% of total U.S. CO_2 emissions.

Natural gas consumption accounted for 265.5 MMT of CO_2 emissions which was 71% of total Residential Sector emissions. The bulk of natural gas usage in the Residential Sector is for heating.

Petroleum, mostly for heating, accounted for 108.0 MMT and 29% of the total Residential Sector emissions.

Natural gas and oil accounted for virtually all CO_2 emissions from the Residential Sector, however, electricity consumed by the Residential Sector accounted for 837.3 MMT of CO_2 emissions in the Electric Sector, or 36% of CO_2 Electric Sector emissions.

Electricity usage in the Residential Sector by usage was approximately: Heating and Air Conditioning (37%), Appliances (40%), Refrigeration (14%), Lighting (9%).[64]

Heating, other than electricity to drive the blower, uses natural gas and oil.

Conservation, discussed in Part III, is the only way to affect CO_2 emissions from natural gas and petroleum in existing homes.

It may be possible to affect heating (and air conditioning) loads in new homes, though there are few options.

- Considerable press is given to using stones and concrete to absorb heat from sunlight and then release the heat after dark. Extra thick insulation, even straw, can reduce heat loss.

- Films or special glass (low E gas filled windows) can reduce heat transfer from sunlight. Homes built underground would, of course, save substantially on heating and air conditioning loads.

89

Alternatives Available for Other Sectors

• Heat pumps, especially in Southern locations, could take advantage of the heat from the earth to reduce natural gas usage and reduce electric consumption for air conditioning.

Organizations have promulgated ways in which to make homes "green," but these often include using materials during construction that are purportedly carbon neutral but do not reduce CO_2 emissions directly.

Conclusion

As the population increases by 139 million, more natural gas and oil will be used in the Residential Sector: CO_2 emissions will likely increase and not decrease.

Reducing CO_2 emissions from the Residential Sector by 80% is highly unlikely.

* * *

Commercial Sector

The Commercial Sector produced 228.8 MMT of CO_2 emissions in 2004, which was 4% of total U.S. CO_2 emissions.

The bulk of CO_2 emissions from this sector were from Natural Gas with 162.7 MMT representing 71% of total CO_2 emissions from this sector. The remaining CO_2 emissions were mostly from petroleum.

The Commercial Sector was also a significant user of electricity and accounted for 795.4 MMT or 35% of CO_2 emissions from the Electric Sector.

Lighting and air conditioning were the primary electric loads in the Commercial Sector.

90

Alternatives Available for Other Sectors

Building owners tend to use the most advanced lighting and air conditioning systems since their cost of operation are substantial and affect profitability. For this reason most office buildings already use fluorescent lighting.

(Builders in the Residential Sector who build on spec frequently use the lowest cost product, so there is some room for improving CO_2 emissions in this area.)

It will be extremely difficult to significantly reduce electric loads in existing commercial buildings.

New buildings may be able to incorporate greater use of natural lighting which could reduce the electric load somewhat. Similarly new office buildings could use special windows (E glass etc.) to reduce heating and air conditioning loads.

So called "Green" building programs establish how to construct eco friendly buildings and some of these suggestions can help reduce CO_2 emissions from new commercial buildings.

Natural gas, the primary source of CO_2 emissions in the Commercial Sector, is primarily used for heating. Conservation is the only way to reduce CO_2 emissions from natural gas in the Commercial Sector, except for improved insulation and use of natural lighting in new buildings.

Conclusion: Commercial Sector

It will be extremely difficult to reduce CO_2 emissions from the Commercial Sector as reductions will have to come largely from conservation.

The growth in jobs in this sector will probably result in increased CO_2 emissions.

Reducing CO_2 emissions by 80% in the Commercial Sector is not likely.

PART THREE

Chapter 11

Conservation

There is considerable reporting in the press about how conservation can eliminate the bulk of CO_2 emissions.

Conservation can play a role in saving energy, but claims about significantly reducing CO_2 emissions are mostly flawed. Part Three addresses the realities about conservation and examines how people overstate the results that can be obtained from conservation.

Conservation is a feel-good alternative, hyped by reporters who have no background in energy technologies.

Electric Sector

Lighting

Lighting represents the greatest opportunity for conservation in the Residential, Industrial and Commercial Sectors, though the Residential Sector may offer the best opportunities.

Industrial and commercial lighting installations are designed to provide the amount of light required to perform tasks efficiently and safely.

Standards have been established for light levels for different surfaces. Machine tool surfaces require 100 foot candles as do desk tops. Some precision applications require much higher levels of lighting while parking lots may only require 15 foot candles. The Illuminating Engineering Society has published tables showing recommended light levels for various tasks.

Reducing these light levels can impede productivity and create unsafe environments.

Conservation

Industry and commercial organizations routinely install the most efficient lighting available during construction. Most commercial buildings (stores, hospitals, office buildings etc.) already use fluorescent lighting wherever possible.[65] Factories also use fluorescent lighting and high energy discharge lighting where fluorescent lighting isn't applicable. When ceiling heights are too high, such as in manufacturing bays, more powerful high intensity discharge (HID) lighting is required.

The only major opportunity for commercial and industrial organizations to reduce electricity usage from lighting will be the emergence of Light Emitting Diodes (LED).[66] LED's have recently been developed that produce white light. Until these recent developments, LED's have been limited to applications where colored lighting is used. For example, LED's are being used in traffic signals to great effect.

While fluorescent lighting reduces electricity usage by around 75% when compared with incandescent bulbs, LED's reduce electricity usage by around 90%. LED's have some serious drawbacks. LED shapes will not fit certain architectural or specialty lighting applications. LED's have not yet been proven suitable for area lighting applications; and it is doubtful LED's will be suitable as replacements for HID lighting.

LED's will, however, be suitable for use in hotels and commercial applications where compact fluorescent bulbs are now used.

LED's are still viewed as a niche product and their costs are about where compact fluorescent bulbs were fifteen years ago, or about $19 for a 100 watt lamp. Costs are falling rapidly with a few lower cost LED lamps already appearing in the market place.

Because industry and commercial organizations already use very efficient lighting, they will have fewer opportunities to achieve significant reductions in electricity usage from lighting through conservation.

Conservation

Residential lighting affords greater opportunities to reduce the use of electricity through conservation.

Replacing incandescent bulbs that burn for a few hours daily, with compact fluorescent bulbs has become the smart thing to do. A 100 watt incandescent bulb uses 100 watts while a compact fluorescent lamp (CFL) rated 100 watts uses only 23 watts of electricity. The lumen output in modern CFL's is about the same as incandescent bulbs. Color rendering has been vastly improved.

Fifteen years ago a 100 watt CFL cost $19. Today, compact fluorescent lamps (CFL) rated 100 watts cost $2. CFL's will often pay for themselves through reduced use of electricity in about two months.[67]

A major drawback to CFL's is that it is very difficult to make them in special shapes, such as flickering candles used in chandeliers. Small R30 spot lights may also be an unsuitable configuration for CFL's. Refrigerator bulbs are an obvious problem. This may pose a major problem to consumers with Congress outlawing incandescent bulbs. (Australia and other countries are also in the process of outlawing incandescent bulbs.)

Most incandescent bulbs in residences are used for only short periods of time, making their replacement with CFL's uneconomic.

Total electricity used for residential lighting was 101 billion kilowatt hours (kWh) in 2001. The EIA had calculated that 35% of this could be saved by replacing incandescent bulbs that burned more than four hours daily with CFL's. This would result in reducing CO_2 emissions by 24 MMT.

If all incandescent lights were replaced with CFL's, 52 MMT of CO_2 could be eliminated.

Population growth would reduce these savings somewhat.

Conservation

A 52 MMT reduction in CO2 emissions is miniscule when compared with the 80% reduction required from the Electric Sector by proposed legislation.

CFL's are the low hanging fruit of conservation. Their first cost is low, the payback is quick and they are easy to install.

Refrigeration

Refrigeration is a large user of electricity in the Residential Sector accounting for approximately 139 MMT of CO2. (This is approximately twice the CO2 of all residential lighting.)

Refrigerators have a high first cost and long payback period when existing refrigerators are replaced with new Energy Star units.

Replacing a 1990's refrigerator with a new unit will reduce its CO2 emissions by around 13%.[68]

In spite of the high cost and long pay back, nearly all refrigerators will be replaced by 2050 because of their average lifespan. It's reasonable to assume that CO2 emissions from refrigerators will be reduced by 20%. (This assumes some continuing improvements in refrigerator efficiency.)

If CO2 emissions for refrigerators are reduced by 20%, it will account for a reduction of 28 MMT CO2.

Other appliances

The life of household appliances is fairly short so it is reasonable to expect that all existing residential appliances (washers, driers, etc.) will be replaced by 2050. (TV's and electronic equipment are not included as household appliances.)

If all other household appliances are replaced with new appliances having a 15% reduction in electricity usage, CO2 emissions would be reduced by 94 MMT. (See Appendix F for calculation)

Conservation

Conclusion: Conservation from Electric Sector.

The conservation efforts itemized above, achieve a reduction of 174 MMT of CO_2, compared with total CO_2 emissions from the Electric Sector of 2,298.6 MMT. This is an 8% reduction compared with the 80% reduction required by proposed legislation.

Economic and population growth will require new office buildings, stores and industrial plants. The increased electric load and CO_2 emissions resulting from growth will be hard to offset with conservation from existing locations.

Conservation is good and improves the nation's productivity, but will play a small role in reducing CO_2 emissions from the generation of electricity.

* * *

Gasoline Sector

As described earlier, the best technology solution for reducing gasoline usage will be to manufacture PHEV's, but what about existing vehicles and those built in the future that are not PHEV's?

Some ideas proposed by Axel Friedrich, one of Europe's top environmental regulators, include; installing stop start systems where the engine is turned off while waiting for stop lights; low rolling resistance tires; and cameras to replace side rear view mirrors that cause wind resistance.[69] Whether people would buy cars with these features without government interference is unknown.

A simple way to reduce gasoline usage is to stop using air conditioning and revert to the 4 and 40 system that was predominantly used before the 1960's; four windows open at 40 mph.

Another way to reduce gasoline usage is to require all drivers to have a pass to automatically pay tolls (e.g. Easy Pass or I Pass) which would eliminate waiting in line with the engine running.

Conservation

Car pooling and teleworking have been promoted for at least twenty years. If they were meaningful solutions they would have been widely adopted by now. It is doubtful that car pooling or teleworking can significantly reduce CO_2 emissions from gasoline.[70]

Another proposal to cut gasoline usage has been to impose a gasoline tax. No one has any information about how high the tax would have to be for people to cut their driving by 10%, or 20% or even 30%. But it would require an 80% reduction to achieve the reductions in CO_2 emissions from gasoline proposed in pending cap & trade legislation.

CAFE standards that would increase gasoline mileage by 20% (from 27.5 mpg to 33 mpg) in current production models would also reduce CO_2 emissions by 20%. While this is a significant reduction, it is likely to be more than offset by increased population. Recently adopted CAFÉ standards will raise the average mileage level to 35.5 mpg by 2016 and may achieve a 30% reduction in CO_2 emissions.

With a combined improvement in gasoline mileage of 20% and increased population of 139 million, CO_2 emissions may <u>increase</u> by about 14%. (The PHEV that can achieve substantial reductions in gasoline usage is considered to be a new technology rather than an effort at conservation.)

(Ethanol is a substitution rather than a conservation method. See Chapter 9)

Conclusion: Conservation from Gasoline Sector

Short of imposing draconian gasoline rationing, it is not feasible to reduce CO_2 emissions from gasoline by 80% through conservation.

An 80% reduction in mileage would result in the average driver only driving 53 miles each week. This would allow the average person to commute to work one day each week.

* * *

98

Conservation

Residential and Commercial Sectors

Natural Gas

Natural gas represented 71% of CO2 emissions from the Residential Sector and 71% from the Commercial Sector, i.e., 265 MMT and 162 MMT of CO2 emissions respectively in 2004.

There are practical steps people can take to reduce residential use of natural gas, oil and electricity.

- Shade trees planted to block sunlight from entering windows can help reduce air conditioning loads. Since these trees would lose their leave in the winter they would allow sunlight to enter in the winter.

- Caulking leaks to prevent heat loss. An infrared camera can see where heat loss is occurring.

- Having the home inspected by the local utility can identify ways to save energy.

Turning down the thermostat to save on heat is a way to save natural gas. Japan has done this and required employees to wear sweaters or coats at work.

Replacing old furnaces could reduce natural gas usage. According to the DOE, 25% of homes have furnaces that are more than 20 years old.

This is another high cost, long payback investment that people will probably defer until the old unit fails. With annual savings of $200 it could take 7 or 8 years to recover the cost of a new Energy Star furnace. While businesses might make the investment (however, they probably wouldn't because of the unsatisfactory ROI) the typical homeowner would not. The typical homeowner is likely to wonder whether the family would move before recovering its investment.

Conservation

If all 25% of old furnaces were replaced with new furnaces having an average improvement in efficiency of 30%, and assuming that natural gas in residential sector is primarily used for heating, CO_2 emissions might be reduced by 20 MMT. 20MMT represents a meager 8% reduction in CO_2 emissions from natural gas in the Residential Sector.

Since most of these old furnaces will fail by 2050, it can be assumed that the 8% reduction will occur. The increase in population will probably offset this reduction.

Though DOE doesn't estimate how many furnaces in the Commercial Sector could be replaced, it might seem reasonable to estimate that another 12 MMT of CO_2 emissions can be eliminated by replacing furnaces in the Commercial Sector.

Replacing single pane with low cost, double pane low e windows will take from 12 to 20 years to return the investment, depending on location. Washington DC may take around 12 years while Chicago Illinois could take 20 years.[71]

In these examples, replacing all the windows in a 2,000 square foot house might reduce natural gas usage by around 25% for the homeowner. If all households that used natural gas for space heating replaced existing windows it might reduce CO_2 emissions in the residential sector by 26 MMT.[72]

It's doubtful that very many homeowners will invest in replacement windows, though the investment could be worthwhile in new construction.

The Waxman-Markey cap & trade bill has a requirement for home inspections of existing homes before they are sold to determine whether they meet required standards. If this provision is maintained in final legislation it might hasten these small savings. How it would affect the sale of existing homes is unknown.

Conservation

Conclusion: Conservation from Residential & Commercial Sectors

It is highly unlikely that conservation can significantly reduce CO_2 emissions from natural gas from the Residential or Commercial Sectors. The estimates shown above might reduce CO_2 emissions from the use of natural gas in the Residential and Commercial Sectors by about 58 MMT.

Total natural gas usage in these sectors accounted for 428 MMT of CO_2 emissions in 2004.

New buildings offer an opportunity to improve energy efficiency through the use of new materials. In the process they will also reduce future CO_2 emissions. Materials such as Eco Rock, a replacement for traditional wall board, can improve energy efficiency.

* * *

Conservation: Rhetoric versus Reality

It's easy to be distracted by the hype surrounding conservation.

News stories and magazine articles talk about the number of coal fired power plants that can be eliminated by taking a specific action, such as replacing incandescent bulbs with compact fluorescent lamps. A less emotional and more accurate representation would be to report the reductions in CO_2 emissions. The mere mention of coal elicits an emotional response unrelated to the amount of CO_2 reductions that can be accomplished by switching to compact fluorescent lamps.

The Sierra Club, for example, has fought against building IGCC power plants that could capture CO_2 emissions merely because the IGCC plant would use coal.[73]

Emotion is a powerful tool for influencing people. For example, Iceland is the poster child for those supporting geothermal energy.

101

Conservation

Roughly two thirds of Iceland's energy comes from geothermal sources. But, the population of Iceland is around 300,000 people or the size of a mid-size American city such as Toledo, Ohio, or Aurora Colorado, or Tampa, Florida.

Iceland should be commended for how it has used its available natural resources, but their experience with geothermal is hardly relevant to a discussion of the energy needs of the United States. As shown earlier, geothermal is scarcely worth mentioning when it comes to the electricity needs of the entire United States.

Another ploy is to claim X pounds of CO_2 emission reductions over the next Y number of years, thereby inflating the numbers.

In addition, reductions in CO_2 emissions from cars do not happen all at once. They are spread out over decades and are offset by population growth.

One commentator blithely suggested that hydrogen should be used in jet airplanes as it burns with fewer CO_2 emissions, completely ignoring there is no practical way to store hydrogen on an airplane.

Then there is the argument based on the question: How do You Eat an Elephant? The answer: One bite at a time!

The inference is that a series of small reductions in CO_2 emissions can add up to achieve an 80% cut in CO_2 emissions. Small improvements in energy efficiency shouldn't be ignored as they do add up and do improve the nation's productivity and competitiveness. But an examination of the magnitude of the CO_2 reductions required from each Sector and the technologies available for making those reductions, demonstrate that it is not possible to achieve an 80% reduction in CO_2 emissions.

The rhetoric leaves the impression that it is easy to achieve huge reductions in CO_2 emissions. Objectivity is required to understand the rhetoric. Each piece of rhetoric should be examined to determine whether it really accomplishes very much and to see whether the technology for achieving the reduction is actually available.

Conservation

For example, people talk about sequestration as though it was a proven technology and a done deal, when, as we have seen, it is not proven and there are many problems that need to be resolved before anyone can say with certainty that sequestration will work on the scale needed.

Chapter 12

Restructuring America

The strongest argument proponents of GHG reductions have for establishing carbon regulations, is that America has high per capita GHG emissions. (See Appendix G for top 25 countries.)

The U.S per capita emissions are more than twice as great as are Europe's.[74]

Is it only a coincidence that the emission reduction environmentalists demand the U.S. make to save the planet – 60% -- is the same as the reduction that would be needed to bring U.S. per capita emissions down to European levels?

At face value it would appear as though Americans are slothful and wasteful.

But, American's have a higher standard of living than Europeans.

The GDP per capita is $43,444 for Americans and only $28,213 for Europeans.[75]

With a GDP 54% higher than Europe's, it would appear as though Americans aren't slothful.

The President of the Czech Republic, the Honorable Vaclav Klaus (an economist by training) recited evidence from the European Union to demonstrate the linkage between CO2 emissions and GDP.

He examined Europe's emission data from 1990 to 2005 and compared this data with the economic growth of three groups of European Countries; those that are less developed, those that were former communist countries and those from "old" Europe.

He found that CO2 emissions were definitely linked to economic growth.[76]

- In Europe's less developed countries – Greece, Ireland, Portugal and Spain- where there has been rapid economic growth from 1990 to 2005, there was a 53% increase in CO2 emissions.

105

Restructuring America

- In the former communist countries where there was a rapid disappearance of heavy industries and a complete economic restructuring and resulting economic decline, CO_2 emissions declined over the same period by 32%.

- "Old" Europe's countries, where there was slow growth or stagnation, CO_2 emissions increased by only 4%. (This calculation excluded Germany because of the impact of East Germany's integration with West Germany.)

Americans, in fact, work harder, longer and smarter than Europeans and have earned their higher standard of living.

Should Americans reduce their standard of living so as to be on a par with European's?

America's higher GDP may not account for all the differences between per capita GHG emissions; there are other differences between America and Europe that also make a difference.

Books have been written examining the geographic and social structures of the U.S. and Europe. There isn't room here to examine all the differences, but it is worth examining some of the differences.

Americans aren't slothful or particularly wasteful as some would claim.

There is no argument that the U.S. and EU are different geographically and structurally. The question is: Should the U.S. change so as to conform to Europe's structure?

Or is it even possible given their contrasting geographies?

Both continents developed differently. Differences can be illustrated by asking people from Europe and the United States about their nationalities. The person from France or Germany or other EU country will answer that he or she is a German, or Frenchman or Norwegian and so forth. The person from Ohio or Arkansas will answer he or she is an American.

Restructuring America

This may not be true for the elite's living in New York City who might say "I'm a New Yorker."

It has only been the last fifty years that European national boundaries have begun to come down.

An American from Chicago thinks nothing of driving to St Louis, Missouri. The Parisian is not likely to drive to Frankfurt, Germany; a comparable distance.

An American thinks nothing about driving from San Francisco to Los Angeles. A person living in Berlin wouldn't readily drive to Brussels; a comparable distance.

An American wouldn't hesitate to drive from New York City to Miami, Florida. The person living in Paris would probably not consider driving to Kiev, the capital of the Ukraine; a comparable distance.

Distances mean much less to Americans who have historically dealt with a continent rather than a small country.

Equally, if not more telling, is the way American cities have evolved.

Metropolitan areas in the United States are spread out. The average person wants to live in a home on a plot of ground owned by him. People commute considerable distances in order to enjoy this lifestyle. It's difficult, for example to ride a bicycle from Sterling Virginia to work in Washington DC, or even to Tysons corner.

European cities are considerably different. A visit to Rotterdam or Copenhagen demonstrates the difference. People live close to their work and can ride their bicycles the few miles it takes to travel the short distance. The following statistic confirms the observation.

- Automobile ownership in the U.S. is 630 per 1,000 people while it is only 340 per 1,000 in Denmark and only 370 per 1,000 in the Netherlands.[77]

Restructuring America

European families are reluctant to move any distance for a new job or opportunity. European families tend to live where their ancestors have lived and owning a piece of land in the suburbs is not as important as in the United States.

European travel patterns have evolved over a few hundred years and, until very recently, have been largely constrained by national boundaries.

For better or worse, where Americans live and work is spread out. Americans have taken advantage of the space the American continent has afforded them. From the very early colonial period, when Americans started to move west to find new land for their families, Americans have viewed space as an asset for development and not something to be horded by the few elite in the ruling class.

As proposed in Europe, government could establish the maximum power for automobiles which would limit the usefulness of SUV's or large sedans but would help curb CO_2 emissions.[78]

Because America is spread out it is difficult to envision a system of railroads to connect Americans to their jobs. The proposed Dulles rail extension along the Dulles corridor is a good example of how a point to point rail system doesn't provide transportation for most people working in Fairfax and Loudon Counties. Metro can take people from one point to another, but most people travel perpendicularly to the rail system to get to work.

New York City is the best example of how a rail system can make a difference in reducing emissions. On Manhattan Island every person lives within walking distance of a subway station. Most cities do not have the same favorable conditions for metro rail or subway systems.

Another proposal emanating in Europe is Community Heating, where steam is generated centrally and then distributed to buildings in the area served by the central heating system. Such a system works best in cities or where living units are built closely together.[79]

Restructuring America

But should the government force Americans to live in cities?

Americans have been large adopters of appliances that reduce work, especially women's work. These appliances use more electricity than doing the work manually.

For example, while 53% of U.S. households owned dishwashers in the 1990's; only 26% in Belgium, 36% in Denmark, 32% in France, 34% in Germany, 18% in Italy, 11% in the Netherlands, 31% in Sweden, 32% in Switzerland and 11% in the U.K. owned dishwashers.[80]

Similarly, while 82% of U.S. households owned a clothes drier; only 39% in Belgium, 30% in Denmark, 12% in France, 17% in Germany, 10% in Italy, 27% in the Netherlands, 18% in Sweden, 27% in Switzerland and 32% in the U.K. owned clothes driers.

Similar disparities exist for Microwaves, VCR's and Personal Computers.

Should American women be required to return to the old days of manual labor?

Another measure of the difference between Americans and Europeans is in the size of their respective living spaces.

The average dwelling space for Americans in 1993 was 712 sq feet per person. For the average European it was 396 square feet per person.[81] (American homes have gotten larger since then.)

Larger living spaces mean more use of energy for heating and air conditioning.

In 1997, 74% of U.S. households had air conditioning.[82] The number of European households having air conditioning is much lower; perhaps as low as 5% in some countries.

Should Americans be required to reduce the size of their homes or block off rooms so they aren't heated or cooled?

Restructuring America

Another European proposal is to "gradually reduce from year to year the amount of energy that energy companies could sell to residential housing."[83] This would force reductions in home size and space used.

To reduce American living standards and reorganize American society is how proponents of GHG reductions envision the process of mandatory reductions in GHG emissions working.

Restructuring America is the ultimate form of conservation.

Without restructuring and changing American society it is impossible to even contemplate how the United States could reduce its CO_2 emissions by 80%.

A plethora of books have been published recently promoting renewable energy.

A few include:

- *Winning our Energy Independence*, by S. David Freeman

- *The Clean Tech revolution* by Pernick and Wilder

- *Freedom from Oil* by Sandalow.

- *Apollo's Fire* by Inslee and Hendricks

These books all have some common threads, including:

1. Demonizing the Oil industry

2. Demonizing Coal

3. Schizophrenia over America's automobile manufacturers while promoting PHEV's

4. Simplistic views of renewables that lack engineering or scientific objectivity.

5. Global warming alarmism.

Restructuring America

If you read one, you have read them all.

The common denominator within these books is their use of global warming to call for restructuring America. They call for a command and control, socialistic economy. "We are on the very cusp of irreversible climactic catastrophe" is the rationale for restructuring America.

Here is what one book says:

> "The policies that I believe are essential require that the federal government take serious and direct action."

> "We have been taken to the cleaners by market forces."

> 'We face a crisis far more severe and deeply embedded in our way of life than the threat of terrorism. To combat it requires us to act ... by passing laws to require what needs to be done."

Here is what another says:

> "For any significant shift to clean technologies to occur, we will need more aggressive public policies ... to place a greater value on activities that reduce GHG's and other pollutants while punishing companies and technologies that increase them."

> "Implement sin taxes"

And another:

> "As we remake the American energy economy, government action is indispensible for setting the rules of the road. ... but its true power will be in harnessing and directing market driven [forces]."

> "The restructuring of the American economy that is needed to bring us industrial-strength clean energy, first requires industrial-strength change in the politics of the country. We need a movement."

Restructuring America

These books all promote a command and control economy. It's important to recognize what that means. Control of development so that single family homes are replaced with multi-use development adjacent to rail lines for transit. More regulations that restrict the use of private property. Big brother and bureaucrats know best. The loss of freedom.

As we have seen in Chapters 8 through 11, there are no "off the shelf" alternatives for cutting CO_2 emissions, certainly not the simplistic proposals contained in the aforementioned books. Restructuring America should not be an acceptable answer.

The loss of freedom shouldn't be allowed.

Research that unleashes breakthrough technologies is the only solution; and a command and control economy inhibits their development.

Chapter 13

Breakthrough Technologies

Wherever they have been tried, command and control economies have produced less than market based economies.

Breakthrough or disruptive technologies emerge from the bottom up, not from the top down. A command and control economy can mobilize huge resources to achieve an objective. The Manhattan project to develop the atomic bomb is an example, as is the Apollo program to put a man on the moon.

In both cases the basic technology was already emerging. The Apollo program needed to build a larger rocket, one that enlarged on the capabilities and performance of the V2 rocket developed by Germany during WWII. The Apollo program needed much better control systems, though the gyroscopic inertial guidance system had already been developed for the Polaris missile.

Kings mandated their alchemists to turn lead into gold. They would have been better served if they had loosened their hold on their economies and allowed innovation to generate economic gold.

Eventually the innovators moved to the colonies and, in later years, to the United States where they unleashed a maelstrom of new ideas, products and industries.

Strong companies can fail by exerting command and control over product development. Competing products seemingly emerge from nowhere to undermine the entrenched corporation.

Disruptive technologies change the name of the game.[84]

These innovations often emerge away from the mainstream. Hydraulics replaced mechanical drives for excavators and unleashed new products that accomplished more for less.

Lighting is another good example.

While it's possible to improve the energy efficiency of the incandescent bulb (and GE claims it has done so) the compact fluorescent lamp, a disruptive technology, achieved a large improvement over the incandescent bulb, and has established a learning curve for the CFL that it has been following since its introduction roughly twenty years ago. Its price has fallen from $19 to $2 over this period.

On a futuristic note, there are huge opportunities for developing breakthrough technologies; game altering technologies that can change all previous assumptions. These are where government should focus its research dollars and where government can provide incentives.

Here are a few ideas of breakthrough and disruptive technologies.

Miniaturized Nuclear Power Plants

It has been reported that the U.S. government laboratory at Los Alamos developed a pocket sized nuclear reactor that is transportable on a truck. It is reportedly safe, has no moving parts, will be sealed at the factory and buried at the point of use. Every seven years or so, it will be returned to the factory for refueling.

The government has licensed Hyperion Power Generation Inc., to manufacture these units. Hyperion forecasts that units will be available in about four years. Presumably this includes obtaining approval from the Nuclear Regulatory Commission.

Being factory built, they could avoid construction problems that accompanied the construction of large nuclear power plants in the past.

Each twenty foot unit will be rated 25 MW and cost around $30 million. To this must be added the cost of the steam turbine generator.

These units are ideally suited for small communities of around 20,000 homes. They could provide power for remote underdeveloped communities in Africa and elsewhere.

114

Breakthrough Technologies

They could also foster the distributed grid, an idea promoted by many people.

These miniaturized nuclear power plants could also threaten the wind energy business. With a probable capacity factor rating of nearly 100%, it would only require around 4,000 of these units to generate 20% of America's electricity.

This compares with the approximately 200,000 wind turbines rated 1.5 MW, having a capacity factor of 30%, which are required to produce the same amount of electricity. In addition the mini nuclear power plants would be base load units, while wind turbines are unreliable and supply power intermittently. (See Wind alternative.)

Additionally, the pocket sized nuclear power plants could be installed near existing transmission lines, thereby eliminating the need for thousands of miles of new transmission lines that are required if wind turbines are built across the wind corridor in mid America.

Jeffrey Immelt, CEO of General Electric Co., bet on wind energy when he bought the business from ENRON. If the miniaturized nuclear power plants are successful, he could lose his bet.

Another important possible usage is to provide heat or electricity for Shell's in-situ process for extracting oil from shale. This could eliminate one of the few environmental issues with respect to the in-situ process. Oil shale could supply all of the oil needs of the United States.

It is unknown whether there will be the same political opposition to mini nuclear power plants as there is toward the larger units.

The Union of Concerned Scientists has already written a letter to the Wall Street Journal objecting to miniature nuclear power plants.[85]

Breakthrough Technologies

Space based power

A recent federal study suggests it may be economically feasible to capture the sun's energy with a satellite and transmit the power to earth.

The report said; "The basic idea is very straightforward: place very large solar arrays into continuously and intensely sunlit Earth orbit (1,366 watts/m squared), collect gigawatts of electrical energy, electromagnetically beam it to Earth, and receive it on the surface for use either as baseload power via direct connection to the existing electrical grid, conversion into manufactured synthetic hydrocarbon fuels, or as low intensity broadcast power beamed directly to consumers."

The report emphasizes that a government "proof of concept" demonstration should be undertaken to act as a catalyst for commercialization of the concept.

This would eliminate the risks and unknowns that would prevent commercial development.

The potential benefits of such a system are huge. It would create a nearly inexhaustible supply of energy and change mankind's dependence on fossil fuels.

The report emphasizes that by "drilling up" rather than "drilling down" the nation can achieve energy security.

Improving the National Grid

Improving the national grid has been a proposal of those supporting cap & trade legislation. It has considerable potential if its focus is on improving the grid rather than masking the high cost of wind power.

Breakthrough Technologies

The national grid needs to be expanded to provide additional capacity and improved reliability. New computer control systems can add to reliability and efficiency.

Those supporting wind power are attempting to include the thousands of miles of additional transmission lines required for transmitting wind generated electricity from remote areas, into a package for improving the national grid, thus masking the true cost of wind generated electricity.

Smart meters, allowing utilities to charge more when their generators are working at their peak and less during off peak hours, would encourage more efficient use of the utilities resources.

Transmission line losses

These losses, also referred to as I^2R losses, waste tremendous amounts of energy while conducting electricity from the power plant to where it is consumed. Inherently they limit the distance that electricity can be transported over copper and aluminum wires.

Energy could be saved if resistance could be eliminated.

Super conductors work in the laboratory, but require very low temperatures so have found few applications outside the laboratory. Similarly, laboratory work is being done on developing transmission lines built from strings of carbon Buckeyballs. MIT has shown how, in the laboratory, carbon nano tubes can conduct electricity with few losses.

Development of low resistance transmission lines would save energy and permit transmitting electricity over greater distances which could, for example, make it more practical to develop solar energy in the Southwest.

Breakthrough Technologies

Storage of electricity

Storage of electricity at a reasonable cost in dollars and space would allow for electricity to be used more efficiently. If a refrigerator sized appliance could be developed to store enough electricity to provide back-up power for an average residence for a day, the distributed grid could become a reality. People would have the choice of either buying electricity from the grid or using the electricity stored in their "storage" appliance; or put another way, they could buy electricity when it is cheapest, which means when it is produced most economically and efficiently.

It would also allow for the efficient use of wind and solar energy, something which is not currently possible.

People have suggested that the batteries in PHEV's could be used as a source of electricity in a distributed grid. Many problems with the idea are obvious. For example, during peak hours when the electricity is needed, cars will be traveling on the road and not parked in a garage connected to the grid; but research in software and grid management could make the idea a reality.

Nuclear fusion

Fusion has been a challenge for over fifty years. The most recent effort is a joint project centered in France where the European Union, the United States, Russia, Japan, South Korea and China are partners in the International Thermonuclear Experimental Reactor (Iter).

Fusion holds the promise of an inexhaustible energy supply without the problems associated with nuclear energy from fission.

Breakthrough Technologies

Magnetic Energy

Science or science fiction? Only research can determine whether Zero-Point Energy or the Casimir effect is real or imagined.

Hydrogen Storage

For hydrogen to be useful in automobiles it must be stored in a form that permits rapid filling of the storage medium (or tank) and rapid release of the hydrogen for use in an engine or fuel cell. Hydrogen storage needs to be at or near room pressures and temperatures. Storage is the major scientific issue that stands in the way of hydrogen replacing gasoline.

* * *

Areas such as these are where government, industry and university laboratories can focus precious research dollars. Industry can largely focus its applied R&D resources on where breakthroughs in science have already occurred and where it's now possible to turn the science into useful products. In the process, if fewer CO_2 emissions occur, so much the better. **But the Holy Grail should be cheap, abundant electricity that can solve many of the world's problems.**

For America, creating economic growth for all Americans, including the 139 million new Americans that will be here by 2050, should be the focus of government, industry and the public.

Crippling the economy with unwise carbon regulations will preclude achieving this objective.

SUMMARY

It's popular these days to say "yes we can", but the laws of physics still can't be repealed.

It's still not possible to turn lead into gold.

Based on the factual information contained in *Carbon Folly*, it is reasonable to conclude it is not possible to cut U.S. CO2 emissions by 80% below 1990 levels; Or by 60%, or by any significant amount. An increase in population virtually precludes cutting CO2 emissions by any significant amount.

The Electric Sector accounts for 39% of total U.S. emissions, so it is critical that CO2 emissions from this Sector be cut by 80% below 1990 levels if there is to be any possibility of cutting total emissions by 80%—or even by 60%.

- As we have seen, nuclear power generation will probably not help cut CO2 emissions. License expirations may require that some nuclear be replaced with coal fired power plants.

- Only demonstration IGCC *Clean Coal* power plants have been built, none with carbon capture capability, so there may be little help from IGCC power plants in cutting CO2 emissions. In addition, if CO2 is captured from IGCC plants it has to be stored underground and large scale underground storage may not prove feasible.

- Existing coal fired power plants will continue to emit CO2 unless a way is found to capture their CO2 emissions, either before combustion, during combustion or afterwards. As yet no system has been proven capable of doing this. And the systems under development require downgrading the power plants modified to capture CO_2 emissions so possibly one additional new power plant must be built for every three plants modified to capture CO_2.

- Sequestering CO_2 underground requires building thousands of miles of pipelines to transport the liquid CO_2. It also requires identifying geologic storage formations that won't leak. Legal and ownership issues haven't started to be addressed and could consume decades before they are settled relative to underground storage.

- Natural gas can reduce CO_2 emissions from coal fired power plants, but requires replacing all coal fired plants with natural gas to achieve a 45% reduction in CO_2 emissions from coal fired power plants. Natural gas is currently a glut but was in short supply before new drilling technologies were developed. Efforts to replace coal with natural gas could result in a shortage of natural gas and increase costs for all users of natural gas, including *home heating*. Drilling in the Gulf of Mexico could improve natural gas supplies.

- Hydro power will probably decline due to several environmental issues, thereby requiring additional CO_2 emission reductions from other power generation sources if the lost power is to be replaced.

  Hydrokinetic units installed in rivers are experimental; but, if successful, could provide an additional source of electricity from renewable sources.

SUMMARY

- Wind power is unreliable and totally inadequate for replacing base load power plants.

- We have seen that other renewables are incapable of supplying anything more than a token increase in electricity.

The Transportation (gasoline) Sector accounts for 20% of total U.S. CO_2 emissions.

- There is insufficient crop land to produce enough ethanol or cellulosic ethanol to replace more than 20% of gasoline. There are ethical issues surrounding using food crops for ethanol, making it essential that cellulosic ethanol be developed if ethanol is to have any effect on gasoline usage.

- Cellulosic ethanol is still in the development phase.

- We have seen that Plug-in Electric Vehicles (PHEV's) have the greatest potential for reducing CO_2 emissions from this Sector.

- PHEV's are still experimental.

- PHEV's, once developed, may be able to reduce CO_2 emissions from gasoline by 18% by 2050.

- Hydrogen powered vehicles are unlikely to become widely available before 2050. Practical on-board storage must be developed before hydrogen can be considered for use in automobiles.

SUMMARY

The <u>Industrial Sector</u> accounts for 18% of total U.S. CO2 emissions.

- Natural gas and oil account for 82% of CO2 emissions from this Sector, but are used for producing product as well as for use in manufacturing processes.

- Industry generally installs the most efficient equipment so there are limited opportunities for making substantial reductions in CO2 emissions by replacing equipment.

- There are always ways to improve processes, so it will be possible to make small reductions in CO2 emissions.

- Achieving substantial reductions in U.S. CO2 emissions requires moving industry off-shore with an accompanying loss of jobs.

The <u>Transportation (excluding gasoline) Sector</u> accounts for 13% of total U.S. emissions.

- Distillates (diesel fuel) account for 56% of the CO2 emissions from this Sector. Diesel fuel is primarily used by the railroads and trucking firms that carry America's products and produce. An increasing population needs food and products, so CO2 emissions from this Sector are likely to increase rather than decrease.

- Jet engines account for 31% of this Sector's emissions. As we have seen, jet engines have been constantly improved so there are limited opportunities for squeezing additional reductions of CO2 emissions from jet engines. Increased population will likely result in more air travel and additional, rather than fewer CO2 emissions.

SUMMARY

The <u>Residential Sector</u> accounts for 6% of total U.S. CO2 emissions.

- With 139 million additional Americans needing places to live and work, the only possible way to reduce CO2 emissions from the Residential Sector is with conservation.

- New building materials may be called green because they create fewer CO2 emissions during their manufacture, but they will not reduce emissions from this Sector. (Reductions would be accounted for in the Industrial or other Sectors.)

- Electric usage from lighting and appliances are accounted for in the Electric Sector. Reductions in CO2 emissions from electricity usage will have to come from conservation.

The <u>Commercial Sector</u> accounts for 4% of total U.S. CO2 emissions.

- Natural gas, which accounts for 71% of this Sector's CO2 emissions, is used primarily for heating. Conservation is the only way to significantly reduce CO2 emissions from this Sector.

- Lighting is accounted for in the Electric Sector. However, commercial office space routinely uses fluorescent lighting so there are few opportunities for significantly reducing CO2 emissions from Lighting. Motion detectors and timers can help reduce the lighting load by eliminating waste.

SUMMARY

Conservation can improve the nation's productivity and is valuable for this reason alone, but conservation cannot reduce U.S. CO_2 emissions by 80% below 1990 levels.

Lighting has the greatest potential for reducing CO_2 emissions from conservation. Compact fluorescent lamps (CFL's) can reduce electric usage for lighting by 75% and CO_2 emissions by a corresponding amount.

- As we have seen, the most optimistic forecast of CO_2 reductions from CFL's is 52 MMT, a fraction of the 4900.8 MMT required to reduce CO_2 emissions by 80%.

Refrigeration is the next largest opportunity for reducing CO_2 emissions from conservation in the Residential Sector.

- As we have seen, the most optimistic forecast of cutting CO_2 emissions by replacing all currently operating refrigerators by 2050 is 28 MMT.

Other household appliances have relatively short operating lives so it is reasonable to assume that all appliances (excluding TV's and electronic equipment) currently in operation will be replaced by 2050 with Energy Star units.

- Replacing all other household appliances with Energy Star appliances by 2050 may reduce CO_2 emissions by as much as 94 MMT.

CO_2 reductions from natural gas by replacing 25% of existing furnaces (those identified as old by the Department of Energy) might result in a reduction of 20 MMT.

These are the low hanging fruit of conservation and taken together they account for less than 4% of the needed reductions in CO_2 to achieve an 80% reduction in CO_2 below 1990 levels by 2050.

Unfortunately these savings will be offset by increased CO_2 emissions from gasoline in spite of conservation efforts, due to more people owning cars.

SUMMARY

This could even be true with a 30% increase in mileage from CAFE or similar standards.

Energy savings for each technology or appliance follows a learning curve, and learning curves are asymptotic. Simply stated, as production doubles, costs decline by a percentage associated with each technology or product. Savings accrue rapidly early in the life cycle but become increasingly more difficult as the product or technology matures.

The only way to achieve major improvements is with breakthrough technologies. A breakthrough technology makes a large improvement and then establishes its own learning curve.

The LED is a new disruptive i.e., breakthrough technology that achieves a substantial improvement over the CFL and will follow a learning curve of its own.

This is why it's possible to say, in so far as most appliances are concerned as well as for many established products and technologies, the low hanging fruit has been picked and savings will become harder to achieve: Until new disruptive technologies emerge.

Conclusions

Based on the preceding it will be impossible to achieve either a 60% reduction in U.S. CO2 emissions below 1990 levels (see Table VI) or an 80% reduction below 1990 levels (see Table VII).

To achieve a 60% reduction below 1990 levels by 2050 requires the U.S. to cut its CO2 emissions by 3905.2 MMT.

To achieve an 80% reduction below 1990 levels by 2050 requires the U.S. to cut its CO2 emissions by 4905.2 MMT

While it's virtually impossible to cut CO2 emissions by 80% (or even by 60%) below 1990 levels by 2050 without restructuring America, it's smart to invest in technologies and products that improve the nation's productivity and energy intensity. (See Appendix I for examples of new technologies.)

60% Reduction U.S. CO2 Emissions from 1990 levels by 2050 (in MMT)			
Source	2004 Actual	Required Reductions From 2004 Actual	2050 60% Target Below 1990 Levels
Electric Generation	2298.6	1577.4	721.2
Gasoline	1162.6	780.5	382.1
Industrial	1069.3	643.8	425.5
Transportation (Excluding Gasoline)	771.1	525.2	245.9
Residential	374.7	238.9	135.8
Commercial	228.8	139.4	89.4
United States Total	5905.1	3905.2	1998.9

Table VI

Total excludes approximately 70 MMT of CO2 emissions from miscellaneous sources.

Source: *Emission of Greenhouse Gasses in the United States 2005* by DOE Energy Information Administration.

MMT = Million Metric Tons

SUMMARY

80% Reduction U.S. CO2 Emissions from 1990 levels by 2050 (in MMT)			
Source	2004 Actual	Required Reductions From 2004 Actual	2050 80% Target Below 1990 Levels
Electric Generation	2298.6	1938.0	360.6
Gasoline	1162.6	971.6	191.0
Industrial	1069.3	856.6	212.7
Transportation (Excluding Gasoline)	771.1	648.2	122.9
Residential	374.7	306.8	67.9
Commercial	228.8	184.1	44.7
United States Total	5905.1	4905.2	999.9

Table VII

Total excludes approximately 70 MMT of CO2 emissions from miscellaneous sources..

Source: *Emission of Greenhouse Gasses in the United States 2005* by DOE Energy Information Administration.

MMT = Million Metric Tons

SUMMARY

Worldwide investment in new technologies and improved energy efficiency will lead to a more prosperous world with the wealth needed to reduce poverty and combat whatever changes in climate, hotter or colder, await us in the future.

Appendix A

Carbon equivalents rather than CO2 emissions

Some will say it is necessary to reduce Greenhouse gasses not just CO2. In other words, if methane, nitrous oxide, HFCs etc. are included in the effort to reduce Greenhouse gasses by 80% it would be easier to achieve that target.

Table VIII shows the carbon equivalents of all Greenhouse gasses, including CO2.

Table VIII		
Gas	MMT Carbon Gas Equivalent	% of Total
CO2	5973.0	84%
Methane	639.5	9%
Nitrous Oxide	353.7	5%
HFCs, PFCs, and SF6	155.9	2%
United States Total	7122	100%

Total includes approximately 70MMT of CO2 emissions from miscellaneous sources.

Source: *Emission of Greenhouse Gasses in the United States 2005* by DOE Energy Information Administration

MMT = Million Metric Tons

Green House Gasses other than CO2 represent a small portion of total Green House Gas emissions.

Appendix A

Agricultural sources represent 182.3 MMT of CO2 equivalents from methane, of which 169.9 MMT comes from livestock. While it's probably difficult to prevent livestock from expounding (some experiments in using different feeds may help), it may be possible to cut 10% from the 54.7 MMT from animal waste by using digesters.

Natural gas systems account for 152.6 MMT of CO2 equivalents from methane.

While it's difficult to cut methane from Agriculture, reduction in natural gas usage in the Electric and Residential Sectors would help reduce methane emissions.

Landfills produced 284.8 MMT of CO2 equivalents from methane. Using this gas for producing electricity reduced methane emissions by 63.3 MMT. Another 58.9 MMT were reduced by flaring. The easy reductions in methane emissions from landfills have already been achieved.

Agriculture accounted for 265.2 MMT of CO2 equivalents from Nitrous Oxide, or 75% of total emissions from Nitrous Oxide.

Conclusions

Not only do these other GHG emissions represent only 16% of the total CO2 equivalents, it will be very difficult to reduce them by 80% below 1990 levels.

Agriculture, for example, is the biggest contributor to these other GHG emissions and represents 40% of their CO2 Equivalent emissions; but, short of doing without meat or corn, agricultural output is bound to increase as the population increases.

Appendix B

Pipelines Required for Sequestering CO2 Emissions
from Coal Fired Power Plants

The following table identifies the coal fired power plants east of the Appalachian Mountains and the number of miles required to transport the CO2 to a geologic formation. The geologic formations used to determine the number of miles are those depicted in the *Carbon Sequestration Atlas of the United States and Canada* published by the Department of Energy's (DOE's) National Energy Technology Laboratory (NETL).

The additional tables show estimates of the number of miles of pipelines required to transport CO2 emissions from all the remaining coal fired power plants 100 MW and larger in the United States (excluding Alaska and Hawaii) to the nearest geologic formation shown in the Atlas.

The following should be noted:

1. Distances are straight line distances and no effort was made to bypass natural geographic obstacles, such as lakes, or to bypass cities.

2. No determination was made as to the maximum amount of liquid CO2 that could be injected at any single point in a geologic formation. Should it be determined that there are limits, the number of miles of pipelines will increase to allow for dividing the pipelines and routing the CO2 to separate injection points.

3. No attempt was made to determine flow rates or the distances that CO2 will migrate from the point of injection. Flow rates could reduce the amount of CO2 that could be injected at any single location. Any limitations on how far CO2 can migrate from the point of injection could limit the capacity of the geologic formation at this location

4. No limits were set as to the maximum amount of liquid CO2 that could be carried by a pipeline. It was assumed the pipeline size could be increased to accommodate the liquid CO2.

5. To minimize the overall length of the pipelines, many coal fired plants had their pipelines routed to an adjoining plant so their combined CO2 could be transported together.

   This assumed that utility companies would not object to transporting CO2 originating at other utilities.

   Liability issue s may prevent combining CO2 flows in this manner.

6. It was assumed that injection points located too close together could cause backpressure and limit flow rates or reduce the amount of CO2 that could be injected at these locations.

   For this reason, injection locations were kept at least 50 miles apart.

7. No effort was made to rank geologic formations as to which might be better at sequestering CO2.

   For this reason Saline Aquifers were used whenever they were closest to coal fired power plants.

   It should be noted that there is a danger that CO2 will combine with the saline water to create carbonic acid that could eat into the surrounding geologic formation to create a point of leakage.

   The Atlas states, "much less is known about saline formations because they lack the characterization experience that industry has acquired through resource recovery from oil and gas reservoirs and coal seams. Therefore, there is a greater amount of uncertainty regarding the suitability of saline formations for CO2 storage."

Appendix B

Coal fired plants east of Appalachian Mountains with pipelines routed to the nearest formations in the Midwest.

Pipeline		Miles
#1	**Main pipeline originating in Boston**	
	12 plants having combined rating of 3,369 MW connected to main pipeline	**951**
#2	**Main pipeline originating in Hudson NY**	
	13 plants having combined rating of 6,411 MW connected to main pipeline	**580**
#3	**Main pipeline originating in Carneys Point NJ**	
	11 plants having combined rating of 4,763 MW connected to main pipeline	**470**
#4	**Main pipeline originating in Morgantown MD**	
	16 plants having combined rating of 9,130 MW connected to main pipeline	**775**
#5	**Main pipeline originating in Sutton NC**	
	14 plants having combined rating of 9,091 MW connected to main pipeline	**715**
#6	**Main pipeline originating in Williams SC**	
	20 plants having combined rating of 12,253 MW connected to main pipeline	**910**
#7	**Main pipeline originating in Bowen GA**	
	13 plants having combined rating of 16,803 MW connected to main pipeline	**605**
	TOTAL **61820 MW**	**5,006**

135

Appendix B

Listings of the remaining coal fired power plants in the United States, excluding Alaska and Hawaii

Coal fired plants located in Midwest, other than Wisconsin and Michigan, with pipelines routed to the nearest Unmineable Coal Seams or Oil & Gas Reservoirs in the Midwest.

Pipeline		# Miles
Goups	122 plants having combined rating of 116,291 MW connected by pipelines	1,611

Coal fired plants located in Michigan with pipelines routed to the nearest Saline formation..

Pipeline		# Miles
Groups	16 plants having combined rating of 14,220 MW connected by pipelines	130

Coal fired plants located in Wisconsin and upper Minnesota with pipelines routed to the nearest Unmineable Coal Seams or Saline formations in the Midwest.

Pipeline		# Miles
9 & 10	39 plants having combined rating of 20,330 MW connected by pipelines	1,761

Coal fired plants located in Iowa, Minnesota, Missouri, Kansas, Oklahoma, & far west Arkansas with pipelines routed to the nearest Unmineable Coal Seams or Saline formations in the far Midwest.

Pipeline		# Miles
Groups	34 plants having combined rating of 20,918 MW connected by pipelines	688

Coal fired plants located in Alabama with pipelines routed to the nearest Unmineable Coal Seam formations.

Pipeline		# Miles
8 & Groups	8 plants having combined rating of 12,448 MW connected by pipelines	245

Coal fired plants located in Florida, Arkansas, Louisiana, Mississippi, east Texas, and south west Oklahoma with pipelines routed to the nearest Unmineable Coal Seam & Saline formations along the Gulf coast.

Pipeline		# Miles
Groups	38 plants having combined rating of 33,215 MW connected by pipelines	346

Appendix B

Coal fired plants located in Florida and Georgia with pipelines routed to the nearest Saline formation in Florida or Georgia.

Pipeline		# Miles
Groups	14 plants having combined rating of 10,806 MW connected by pipelines	240

Coal fired plants located in the Rocky Mountain states of North Dakota, north west South Dakota, Montana, Wyoming, Colorado, Texas, New Mexico, Utah, Arizona and portions of Kansas with pipelines routed to the nearest Unmineable Coal Seam or Saline formation.

Pipeline		# Miles
Groups	42 plants having combined rating of 32,845 MW connected by pipelines	630

Coal fired plants located along the west coast with pipelines routed to the nearest Saline formation.

Pipeline		# Miles
Groups	5 plants having combined rating of 3,391 MW connected by pipelines	156

Appendix C

Geothermal Power[86]

Approximately 20 geothermal plants in the United States with a total rating of 3,233 MW generate 0.36% (three point six tenths of one percent) of total US electricity. Geothermal resources currently identified in the United States could provide a total of 20,000 MW of capacity which is equal to 2% of total electric generating capacity in the US.

In addition to the existing 2,800 MW of installed capacity, there are 285 MW currently under construction with the potential for another 1,000 MW over the next ten years. Areas being explored for commercial viability could add some additional capacity by 2020. Realistically, US geothermal generating capacity in 2020 could reach 5,000 MW

Supporters of geothermal power say that undiscovered resources could produce five times the current capacity. It may be worth exploring for such resources, but unless they are found very quickly, they will have little impact on providing electricity before 2020.

"Hot dry rock" is a more futuristic proposal where fluids are pumped deep into the earth to create steam from the very hot rocks located well below the earth's surface. In 2003, an Australian company completed drilling its first well to a depth of 14,405 feet to reach hot rock having a temperature of 560 degrees F. A second well is being drilled. This is a pioneering effort at hot dry rock geothermal electricity production in Australia.

Geothermal electricity is generated using three methods.

- Direct Steam

  Direct steam uses high temperature steam as it emerges from the earth to drive a turbine generator. These are the most cost effective plants but sites with steam are rare.

139

Appendix C

- Flash Steam

    Flash steam systems inject high temperature brine (above 400 °F) from the earth into a low-pressure chamber where the brine flashes directly into steam; where the steam drives a turbine generator.

- Binary cycle

    The binary cycle method passes moderate temperature brine (below 400 °F) through a heat exchanger where its heat is transferred to another fluid which vaporizes; where the vaporized fluid drives a turbine generator.

Moderate temperature brine is the most common geothermal resource so binary cycle plants will be the most common.

The cost of producing geothermal electricity is between 5 and 8 cents per KWHr (versus 2.3 to 3 cents for fossil fuel generated electricity). It will be difficult to lower this cost significantly since these installations use established technologies (heat exchangers, turbines and electric generators) in traditional ways. Drilling and exploration represents 24% to 50% of the cost so new drilling technologies may help slightly lower the cost of new plants.

The amount of energy available from a geothermal source gradually declines, though reinjection of fluids can help preserve the fluid volume of the reservoir and the reservoir should outlive the useful life of the equipment.

Other Geothermal Possibilities

Other uses of geothermal heat do not generate electricity but can help reduce the need for electricity. They are mentioned here solely to ensure complete coverage.

Appendix C

Geothermal Heat Pumps

These systems use shallow ground energy to heat and cool buildings.

The upper 10 feet of the Earth's surface maintains a nearly constant temperature of 50 to 60° F. A geothermal heat pump system consists of pipes buried in the ground near a building, connected to a heat exchanger and ductwork in the building. In winter, heat from the relatively warmer ground goes through the heat exchanger into the house. In summer, hot air from the house is pulled through the heat exchanger into the relatively cooler ground.

Direct-Use Piped Hot Water

Hot water taken directly from hot springs can be used to heat buildings, melt ice and grow plants.

Appendix D

Solar Power[87]

Solar currently supplies around 0.1% (one tenth of one percent) of US power requirements with little prospect of supplying more than 0.1% in the near future.

To grasp the small likelihood of widespread use of solar power over the next forty years, it is necessary to examine each of the solar power technologies. Broadly speaking, they are either used for local (home or commercial buildings) or centralized generation of electricity.

Local (i.e. home) generation of electricity uses photovoltaic cells that convert sunlight into electricity where cells are typically located on rooftops. Solar energy is also used in thermal and passive systems for heating water and buildings. Thermal and passive can reduce the need for generating electricity but their effect in this regard is negligible.

Centralized technologies use Concentrating Solar Power techniques. The three centralized systems currently under development are:

- Parabolic troughs

- Power towers

- Dish-engine

Photovoltaic Power in the United States

The cost of a photovoltaic power supply for a residential house is between $10,000 and $40,000, depending on the amount of power required by the owner. The average household usage of electricity in the US in 2000 was 11,400 KWHrs, which includes urban apartments etc. A typical single family home could expect somewhat lower usage unless the home is heated by electricity. Individual homeowners can determine their usage from their electric bills.

Appendix D

The amount of electricity produced by a system depends on the amount of sunlight and its intensity. Insolation is the measure of sunlight intensity in KWHr/Meter. A 600 square foot, roof mounted solar panel in Baltimore might generate 3,650 KWHrs of power during a year while a similar system in Arizona might produce more than twice this much power. Costs therefore will vary widely depending on location. Generally speaking, the cost of photovoltaic electricity is between $.20 and $1.00 per KWHr versus the average residential price for electricity of $.08 per KWHr.

There are government subsidies that vary by state that are intended to help foster the use of photovoltaic solar. In addition, some states permit "Net Power". "Net Power" can permit the owner of a photovoltaic system to sell excess power to the local utility at the same price the homeowner pays the utility, in effect reversing the direction of the electric meter when the home owner is using less power than is being generated by the photovoltaic system.

Even with subsidies and "Net Power", the economics of photovoltaic power are nearly always unattractive (with negative cash flows) and precludes widespread use of photovoltaic solar power.

So called second and third generation photo voltaic processes (e.g., plastic sheet) are still less efficient than silicon cells, though they may possibly be more cost effective.

The efficiency of solar cells will have to improve substantially before photovoltaic generation has any possibility of becoming cost competitive.

Concentrating Solar Power Technologies:

These technologies use mirrors to concentrate sunlight to up to 5,000 times its normal intensity.

Parabolic trough systems use linear parabolic concentrators to focus sunlight on a receiver tube filled with heat-transfer oil. The heated oil passes through a heat exchanger to create steam, which turns a turbine generator…similar in this respect to traditional power generation.

Power towers use sun-tracking mirrors, called heliostats that focus the sunlight onto a receiver mounted on top of a tower. The solar heat is collected in a nitrate-salt fluid that is used to generate steam (as above) using a conventional turbine generator to produce electricity. The salt solution can store the heat energy for a period of time so that the turbine generator can be run after sunlight is no longer available.

Both the parabolic trough and power tower systems can be operated as hybrid systems using natural gas when sunlight is not available. Both are intended for use as large scale units rated 30 MW or above.

Dish engine systems use a parabolic dish with mirrors to focus the sunlight onto a receiver mounted on the dish (similar to a radar dish). Fluid in the receiver is heated to around 1,400 degrees F, which is used to generate electricity in a small engine connected to the receiver. The most common type of heat engine used in this system is the Stirling engine. The primary advantage of the dish-engine system is that it is relatively small, rated 10 to 50 KW, and can possibly be grouped as modules to form a large system.

All three of these CSP technologies (parabolic trough, power tower and dish-engine) are still under development. There are nine parabolic trough systems with a combined rating of 354 MW that have operated successfully in California. There is a power tower system under test in Southern California. Several prototype dish-engine systems have been built but do not have sufficient operating experience to indicate they are beyond the experimental stage.

Theoretically, a 100 MW power tower could be built on less than 1,000 acres (approximately 1.5 square miles) of vacant land in the Southwest. However, this technology is still in the developmental stage with many questions still to be answered, not the least of which is cost.

Appendix D

Electricity produced by these three systems reportedly costs from over 11 cents /kWh to 18 cents / kWh, which is 4 to 7 times more costly than conventionally generated electricity. Projected costs for 2020 remain over 4 cents per kWh.

There are reports that actual costs per kWh on systems in operation are considerably higher than these.

The Department of Energy forecasts that none of these technologies will be competitive with conventional power generation until well past 2020. A review by A. D. Little indicates there is no compelling reason to believe that the current cost of $200 - $250 /M^2 for the concentrator optics (the single most important cost elements for these systems) can be reduced by 50% (let alone the 75% reduction that seems to be necessary to make these systems competitive).

Concentrating Solar Power technologies are in the developmental stage. A few additional developmental systems may be built between now and 2020. In spite of their theoretical ability to supply large blocks of power, power towers, or any concentrating solar power technology, will have little if any effect on our use of fossil fuels before 2020; and possibly long after that. They have enough potential however to warrant continued research and development

DC Transmission of Solar Power.

The suggestion has been made to produce huge amounts of solar power in the Southwest and then transmit it around the United States using HVDC transmission lines installed along Interstate highway rights of way.[88] The proposal assumed that solar power can be produced at night or otherwise stored so as to displace coal fired power plants.

The proposal assumed there are proven technologies available for such an approach.

Appendix D

There are several issues that have not been fully analyzed so, though the proposal is interesting, one cannot assume that the technologies are ready for the intended application of carrying most of the nations' electricity from the Southwest to distant points throughout the country.

1. Line losses.

   AC transmission carries a very large penalty in the form of line losses. Offsetting this negative is that AC power is typically produced near the point where it is consumed so that line losses are kept to as low a level as possible.

   While HVDC line losses are substantially less than AC line losses, the distances being proposed for HVDC transmission will result in large line losses, especially when transmitting power to the East Coast or to New England. Whether these losses would adversely affect the proposal needs to be evaluated.

2. Distances:

   The largest HVDC transmission line in the world is the Itaipu project in Brazil with a transmission distance of 988 miles, with an operating voltage of 600kV. In the U.S. there is a 488 mile long HVDC Intermountain transmission line to Los Angeles.

   The distance from Arizona to New York is around 2,500 miles, to Cleveland is around 2,000 miles, and to Seattle is around 1,600 miles.

   Building multiple lines at these distances has never been done and needs to be evaluated.

3. Size:

   Total installed U.S. utility owned generating capacity was approximately 1,000,000 MW in 2005. The Itaipu HVDC transmission line was rated at 6,300 MW. Most HVDC lines are considerably smaller.

147

Appendix D

The proposal to transmit all of U.S. electricity from the Southwest could require as many as one hundred HVDC transmission lines.

The estimated cost of the proposal was $420 billion which appears to be fairly accurate if interstate highway rights of way could be utilized. As shown below, this is not possible so the cost of acquiring rights of way must be added to the $420 billion.

4. Rights of way.

The proposal assumes that the HVDC transmission lines could be built using interstate highway rights of way. There are only two or three interstate highways emanating from the Southwest where the solar power plants would be installed. Obviously these are not adequate to accommodate the large number of HVDC transmission lines.

There are only five interstate highways that run from the West to the East Coast of the United States. These too are inadequate for handling all the HVDC transmission lines required for getting the electricity to the Eastern half of the United States.

In any event, it's also doubtful that HVDC transmission lines could be built along these rights of way for a number of space and safety reasons.

It would seem to be unwise to embark on a $420+ billion program to build HVDC transmission lines until it is certain that losses, distances and the need to obtain rights of way do not undermine the proposal; and more importantly, a way is found to generate electricity at night using solar and to also find a practical way to store electricity.

148

Appendix E

Estimate of CO2 emissions when 75% of vehicles are PHEV's

1. To calculate the amount of electricity required to recharge batteries based on miles driven.

   Multiply the energy required for recharging[89] times the miles driven. Multiplying the result by the number of PHEV's forecast for 2050 gives an estimate for the amount of kWh per year required to recharge PHEV's

   0.33 kWh/mile x 12,000 miles/year = 3,960 kWh/year/vehicle

   3,960 kWh/year/vehicle x   240,750,000 PHEV vehicles in 2050 =

   953,370,000,000 kWhr/year for charging batteries

2. To estimate the share of electricity required for recharging PHEV's as a percentage of total kilowatt hours generated in the U.S., divide the kWhr for recharging by total U.S. kWhr.

   953,370,000,000 kWhr/year / 4,054,688,000,000 kWh US Generation 2004 = 23.5%

3. To estimate the amount of CO2 that will be emitted by generating the electricity used for recharging PHEV's, multiply U.S. CO2 emissions in 2004 by the percentage of electricity required for recharging batteries. This assumes that the mix of fuels remains the same in 2050 as in 2004 so represents an approximation of CO2 emissions for recharging PHEV's.

   2,229 MMT CO2 Electric Sector emissions in 2004 x 23.5 % = **540** MMT of CO2 from charging batteries

Appendix E

4. To estimate the CO2 emissions from gasoline by the 25% of cars in 2050 that are not PHEV's, calculate projected CO2 emissions in 2050 if all vehicles were not PHEV's[90]

   1,162 MMT emissions from Gasoline in 2004 x (223,000,000 Number of vehicles 2004 / 321,000,000 Number vehicles 2050) = 1,673 MMT prorated increase in CO2 emissions from more vehicles in 2050

5. To estimate the CO2 emissions in 2050 from the 25% of vehicles that are not PHEV's

   25.0% Percentage of vehicles using gasoline in 2050 x 1,673 MMT = **418** MMT from gasoline used by 25% of vehicles

6. To calculate total estimated CO2 emissions in 2050 when 75% of all vehicles are PHEV's

   540 MMT + **418** MMT = **959** MMT Total CO2 emissions

Appendix F

Calculation for CO2 emissions from all other household appliances after Lighting and Refrigeration.

1. Using the total CO2 emissions from electricity usage by the Residential Sector, subtract the CO2 emissions associated with lighting and the CO2 emissions associated with refrigeration to determine the balance of CO2 emissions from electricity usage in the Residential Sector.

    837.3 MMT CO2 from total Residential electricity usage

    - 69.0 MMT for Residential Lighting 2004

    - 139.0 MMT for Refrigeration 2004

    629.3 MMT balance 2004

2. Assuming a 15% reduction in CO2 emissions from all other uses of electricity in the Residential Sector, multiply the balance determined above by 15%

    15% Estimated reduction for all remaining Residential Electric   x   629.3 MMT = **94.4** MMT reductions in additional CO2 emissions.

    Note: Excludes TV's and other electronic appliances.

Appendix G

GHG Emissions of Top 25 Countries

(UN data, except as noted.)

Country	Latest Data	Total Emissions	MMT per Capita
Jamaica	1994	116.23	47.44
Bahrain	1994	19.47	34.34
Belize	1994	6.34	30.50
Paraguay	1994	140.46	29.85
Luxembourg	2004	12.72	27.71
Australia	2004	529.23	26.54
United States	2004	7067.6	23.92
Canada	2004	758.07	23.72
Grenada	1994	1.61	19.22
New Zealand	2004	75.09	18.82
Ireland	2004	68.46	16.78
Estonia	2004	21.32	15.97
Finland	2004	81.43	15.55
Barbados	1997	4.06	15.34
Czech Republic	2004	147.11	14.38
Belgium	2004	147.87	14.22
Trinidad & Tobago	1990	16.39	13.49
Netherlands	2004	218.09	13.44
Kazakhstan	1994	219.24	13.14
Denmark	2004	69.62	12.86
Turkmenistan	1994	52.31	12.74
Cameroon	1994	165.73	12.69
Israel	2000	75.24	12.45
Greece	2004	137.63	12.40
Germany	2004	1015.3	12.28

For Comparison. EU estimate from other sources:
EU 15   11.1

Appendix H

Next Generation Nuclear Technologies

Two factors have affected the deployment of new nuclear power plants in the United States; safety and storage of spent nuclear fuel.

Three Mile Island was the worst nuclear accident in the United States and is foremost in the minds of many.

At Three Mile Island, 90% of the fuel rods ruptured yet there was little radiation exposure of the public. Certainly, there were no deaths. "The maximum exposure to the nearest member of the public was little more than 1/3 of the NRC's annual limit for the public." And, no worker exceeded the commission's current limit of 5 millirems per year for occupational exposure.

Spent reactor fuel is currently stored on-site at existing nuclear power plants. Plans for a permanent storage facility at Yucca Mountain in Utah have been virtually stopped by the Obama administration. Legal action to stop development of the site which is intended as the permanent storage facility for spent fuel continues.

Some organizations have claimed there is significant danger associated with shipping spent fuel to Yucca Mountain.

The navy's experience with shipping fuel from its 100 reactors has been exemplary. "New nuclear fuel has been processed, fabricated, and safely shipped across the U.S. for nearly 50 years. Spent fuel from U.S. nuclear ships is routinely and safely shipped to storage sites."

France has reprocessed its spent nuclear fuel without incident.

Cost could now be a factor in proceeding with new nuclear reactors.

France's nuclear reactor company AREVA, has experienced delays and cost increases at Olkiluoto, Finland for its first of a kind next generation reactor. Greenpeace had claimed there were insufficient qualified supervisors overseeing the welding and this required AREVA to send specialized personnel to Finland.

155

Appendix H

AREVA experienced large increases in material costs. In total, AREVA could experience a 50% increase in costs and a two year delay in completing the plant.

AREVA has taken steps in the United States to establish a manufacturing capability in the United States, recognizing that America's nuclear manufacturing capability has atrophied over the past 25 years.

AREVA intends to build one third of the new nuclear power plants proposed for the United States. It has entered into a joint agreement with Northrop Grumman Corporation's, Newport News shipbuilding facility to engineer and manufacture heavy components for AREVA's EPR nuclear design. It has also worked with Lehigh Heavy Forge in Bethlehem, Pa., to produce forgings for the U.S. EPR.

Interference by activists will also likely be a factor in the U.S. when new nuclear plants are built.

Material costs have increased substantially during the past few years, but the recent downturn could result in a lowering of costs from the levels experienced by Areva in Finland.

Delays caused by legal actions against nuclear power plants were a major problem in the 1960's and 1970's and could be a problem again. Delays are a major cause of cost increases.

This is the backdrop facing the construction of next generation nuclear power plants in the United States.

Here is a description of these plants.

Appendix H

The following details of next generation nuclear technologies has been prepared by

G. Neil Midkiff

New Nuclear Power Designs[91]

Any new reactor built in the United States over the next decade or so would most likely use designs either recently certified by the Nuclear Regulatory Commission (NRC) or that will be certified by the NRC in the near future. (Design approval can alternatively coincide with construction and operation licensing, skipping the certification process.) The re-creation of older designs is popular overseas and cannot be ruled out in the United States.

Presently there are three certified new reactor designs in the United States: the System 80+, the Advanced Boiling Water Reactor (ABWR), and the AP600. These designs are sometimes called Advanced Light Water Reactors (ALWR) because they incorporate more advanced safety concepts than the reactors previously offered by vendors.

They are also sometimes called **Generation III reactors** to distinguish them from earlier designs now operating in the U.S. and globally and from later designs now seeking certification which are sometimes called **Generation III plus**. Design certifications can expire if not supported by a vendor.

The following are more detailed descriptions of each of the reactor designs.

Appendix H

Generation III Reactor Designs

System 80+ (Westinghouse BNFL):

The System 80+ reactor is a Pressurized Water Reactor (PWR) designed by Combustion Engineering (CE) and by CE's successor owners ABB and Westinghouse BNFL. The NRC has certified the System 80+ for the U.S. market, but Westinghouse BNFL no longer actively promotes the design for domestic sale. The System 80+ provides the basis for the APR1400 design that has been developed in Korea for future deployment and possible export.

Information on the System 80+ reactor can be found on http://www.nei.org/index.asp?catnum=3&catid=703 and http://www.nuc.berkeley.edu/designs/sys80/sys80.html

ABWR (General Electric, Toshiba, Hitachi):

Among the three NRC- certified ALWR designs only the ABWR has been deployed. Three ABWRs operate in Japan, and three are under construction, two in Taiwan and one in Japan. While the ABWR design is usually associated in the United States with General Electric, units now being built in Japan are products of Toshiba and Hitachi. Toshiba, and Hitachi frequently associate with General Electric in possible ABWR projects in the U.S. There are many variations in ABWR design. The most frequently mentioned capacities are in the 1250-1500 MWe range though smaller and larger designs have been proposed depending on the vendor. Vendors now claim costs for building the ABWR that are low enough that they have attracted some customer interest. Information on the ABWR can be found at http://www.nei.org/doc.asp?docid=110.

Appendix H

AP600 (Westinghouse BNFL):

The AP600 is a 600 MW PWR certified by the NRC. The AP600, while based on previous PWR designs, has innovative passive safety features that permit a greatly simplified reactor design. Simplification has reduced plant components and should reduce construction costs. The AP600 has been bid overseas but has never been built. Westinghouse has deemphasized the AP600 in favor of the larger, though potentially less expensive (on a kilowatt basis) AP1000 design.

Comments re Advanced Light Water Reactors

The initial ALWR designs as a group have been praised for their improvements in reactor safety and simplicity, but construction costs on a "per kilowatt of capacity" basis might remain a barrier to commercial success in the U.S. The ABWR design however has many variations and continues to be selectively promoted by several vendors.

Generation III + Reactor Designs

AP1000 (Westinghouse):

Quite often when a reactor is named, its name includes digits such as the "1000" in the AP1000. This usually indicates the initial electricity generating capacity of the design, in this case 1000 MWe. Seldom do the digits indicate the present design capacity as the design evolves.

The most recent AP1000 design has been bid in China with a 1175 MW-capacity. The AP1000 is an enlargement of the AP600, designed to almost double the reactor's target output without proportionately

159

increasing the total cost of building the reactor. Westinghouse anticipates that operating costs are anticipated to be below the average of reactors now operating in the United States.

While Westinghouse BNFL owns rights to several other designs, the AP1000 is the principal product that the company now promotes in the United States for near term construction. The AP1000 is a PWR with innovative, passive safety features and a much simplified design intended to reduce the reactor's material and construction costs while improving operational safety.

One consortium of nine utilities called NuStart Energy promotes the AP1000 in the United States and has informed the NRC that it intends to apply for a combined construction and operating license (COL) for the design. This is not a commitment to build the design.

Westinghouse submitted a bid in early 2005 to build as many as four AP1000s at two sites in China. Information on the AP1000 can be found at http://www.nei.org/doc.asp?docid=770.

ESBWR (Economic Simplified, Boiling Water Reactor) (General Electric):

The ESBWR (1500 MWe) is a new simplified BWR design promoted by General Electric and some allied firms.

The ESBWR constitutes an evolution and merging of several earlier designs including the ABWR that are now less actively pursued by GE and other vendors beyond the exceptional case of Bellefonte in Alabama.

The intent of the new design, which includes new passive safety features, is to cut construction and operating costs significantly from earlier ABWR designs. GE and others are investing heavily in the ESBWR though the design might not be available for deployment for several years. The ESBWR's builders however anticipate that the design will be available in time to meet any potential construction targets in the U.S. The nine-utility NuStart Energy group promotes the ESBWR as well as the AP1000 design. NuStart has informed the NRC that it intends to apply for a COL for the ESBWR in addition to any AP1000 application. Dominion Resources is also evaluating the ESBWR for its North Anna plant in Virginia but has not declared its COL intentions for the design.

European Pressurized Water Reactor (EPR) (Areva NP):

Areva NP announced in early 2005 that it would market its EPR design (1600 MWe) in the United States and has recently begun pre-certification activities. The U.S.-market version is called the Evolutionary Pressurized Water Reactor.

The EPR is a conventional, though advanced, PWR in which components have been simplified and considerable emphasis is placed on reactor safety.

The design is now being built in Finland with a target commercialization during 2010. The French government has also authorized building an EPR at Flamanville 3 in France. Additional EPRs might replace additional commercial reactors now operating in France starting in the late 2010s and EPRs have been bid, in China and elsewhere.

The proposed size for the EPR has varied over time, but is most frequently placed around 1600 MWe. Earlier designs were as large as 1750 MWe. The EPR is promoted in the United States by UniStar Nuclear, a joint venture of Constellation Energy and AREVA NP.

UniStar is presently looking at the possibility of building EPRs at Constellation-owned sites at Nine Mile Point and Calvert Cliffs and has had discussions with other firms. Areva NP anticipates submitting a design certification application to the Nuclear Regulatory Commission during late 2007 or early 2008.

(Constellation was recently purchased by a Buffett company.)

Appendix H

US-APWR (Mitsubishi Heavy Industries)

The US-APWR (1700 MWe) is a U.S.-marketed variation on APWR design sold in Japan by Mitsubishi Heavy Industries. The 1538 MW APWR has been selected by Japan Atomic Power Company for two units to be located at Tsuruga in Japan with the first unit slated for completion in 2014.

Other Japanese generating companies are also interested in the APWR design. The 1700 MW US-APWR was only recently (June 2006) announced for the U.S. market and is not presently being certified in any other international markets.

The US-APWR has not yet received publicized support from any U.S. generating company. Pre-application design certification activities before the U.S. Nuclear Regulatory Commission began during July 2006. Mitsubishi targets a design certification application for March 2008 and hopes complete the process during 2011. Mitsubishi also wants to have the reactor available for construction in the U.S. as early as 2011. Mitsubishi is also investigating certifying a second, smaller reactor design at a capacity of 1200 MW.

Further Information can be found at
http://www.mhi-ir.jp/english/new/sec1/200607031122.html.

ACR700 (Atomic Energy of Canada Limited):

AECL's "Advanced CANDU Reactor" ACR70016 has been developed over a lengthy period of time and is considered by its vendor to be an evolution from AECL's internationally successful CANDU line of PHWRs.

CANDU reactors and their Indian derivatives have been more of a commercial success than any other line of power reactors except the LWRs.

One of the innovations in the ACR700, compared to earlier CANDU designs, is that heavy water is used only as a moderator in the reactor. Light water is used as the coolant. Earlier CANDU designs used heavy water both as a moderator and as a coolant. This change makes it debatable whether the ACR700 is a PHWR, a PWR, or a hybrid between the two designs.

AECL has aggressively marketed the ACR700 offering low prices, short construction periods, and favorable financial terms. As is the case for most non-LWR reactors, most U.S. utilities, nuclear engineers, and regulators have only limited working familiarity with the design. Interest was initially shown by Dominion Resources regarding possible construction at North Anna (Virginia) as well as by utilities in several international locations, notably in Canada and the United Kingdom.

Dominion has recently switched to the ESBWR design for North Anna in anticipation of the slow regulatory approval process for the innovative Canadian design. AECL has subsequently slowed its efforts to certify the ACR700 in the United States though the firm still intends to begin the certification process toward the end of 2005. AECL announcements indicate increased interest in a larger ACR1000 design.

Pebble-bed Modular Reactor (PBMR) (Eskom):

The PBMR, which uses helium as a coolant, is part of the HTGR family of reactors and thus a product of a lengthy history of research, notably in Germany and the United States.

More recently the design has been promoted and revised by the South African utility Eskom and its affiliates. Westinghouse BNFL is a minority investor. Prototype variations of the PBMR are now operating in China and Japan.

Eskom has received administrative approval to build a prototype PBMR in South Africa, but has also been delayed in implementation by judicial rulings regarding the reactor's potential environmental impact. Certification procedures in the U.S. have slowed, but never have been abandoned.

At around 165 MWe the PBMR is one of the smallest reactors now proposed for the commercial market. This is considered a marketing advantage because new small reactors require lower capital investments than larger new units. Several PBMRs might be built at a single site as local power demand requires.

Small size has been viewed as a regulatory disadvantage because most licensing regulations (at least formerly) required separate licenses for each unit at a site. The NRC also does not claim the same familiarity with the design that it has with LWRs.

Fuels used in the PBMR would include more highly enriched uranium than is now used in LWR designs. The PBMR design is considered a possible contender for the U.S. Department of Energy's Next Generation Nuclear Plant (NGNP) program in Idaho. China has also indicated interest in building its own variation of the PBMR. China and South Africa have also discussed cooperation in their efforts.

Details regarding the PBMR design can be found on https://www.pbmr.com/. Information related to certification of the PBMR can be found at

http://www.nrc.gov/reactors/new-licensing/design-cert/pbmr.html

Gas-turbine Modular Helium Reactor (GT-MHR) (General Atomic):

The GT-MHR is an HTGR design developed primarily by the U.S. firm, General Atomic. The most advanced plans for GT-MHR development relate to building reactors in Russia to assist in the disposal of surplus plutonium supplies. Parallel plans for commercial power reactors would use uranium-based fuels enriched to as high as 19.9 percent U-235 content. This would keep the fuel just below the 20 percent enrichment that defines highly enriched uranium.

Appendix H

In initial GT-MHR designs, the conversion of the energy to electricity would involve sending the heated helium coolant directly to a gas turbine. There has been concern regarding untested, though non-nuclear aspects of this generation process. This has led potential sponsors to advocate similar ideas involving less innovative heat transfer mechanisms prior to generating electricity or commercial heat.

The U.S. utility, Entergy, has participated in GT-MHR development and promotion and has used the name "Freedom Reactor" for the design. Because coolant temperatures arising from HTGRs are much higher than from LWRs, the design is viewed as an improved commercial heat source.

There has been particular attention paid to the design's potential in the production of hydrogen from water. The GT-MHR is considered a potential contender for the US Department of Energy's Next Generation Nuclear Plant (NGNP) program.

Information on the GT-MHR can be found on http://www.ga.com/gtmhr/ Information related to certification of the GT-MHR can be found at http://www.nrc.gov/reactors/new-licensing/design-cert/gt-mhr.html.

International Reactor Innovative and Secure (IRIS) (Westinghouse BNFL led consortium):

Westinghouse BNFL has promoted the IRIS reactor design as a significant simplification and innovation in PWR technology. The reactor design is smaller than most operating PWRs and would be much simplified. The IRIS reactor includes features intended to avoid loss of coolant accidents. Pre-certification is proceeding. The IRIS reactor may show potential during the next decade. Certification could precede commercial availability. IRIS has a targeted 2010 certification completion date. IRIS presently has no utility sponsor in the U.S.

Appendix H

Generation IV Designs

The U.S. Department of Energy participates in the Generation IV International Forum (GIF), an association of thirteen nations that seek to develop a new generation of commercial nuclear reactor designs before 2030. The U.S., Canada, France, Japan and the United Kingdom signed an agreement on February 28, 2005 for additional collaborative research and development of Gen IV systems.

Criteria for inclusion of a reactor design for consideration by the initial GIF group include:

1. Sustainable energy (extended fuel availability, positive environmental impact);

2. Competitive energy (low costs, short construction times);

3. Safe and reliable systems (inherent safety features, public confidence in nuclear energy safety); and

4. Proliferation resistance (does not add unduly to unsecured nuclear material) and physical protection (secure from terrorist attacks).

GIF members agreed during 2002 to concentrate their efforts and funds on six concept designs whose goal is to become commercially viable between 2015 and 2025. There is thus some leeway between the 2030 target for the GIF program implementation and the targets for individual concepts. Individual GIF participant nations are free to pursue any individual technology they choose. The United States intends to pursue each design.

The GIF group, along with the U.S. Department of Energy's Nuclear Energy Research Advisory Committee (NERAC), published "A Technological Roadmap for Generation IV Nuclear Energy Systems" (December 2002) which summarizes plans and designs for generation IV projects. Each design is evolutionary; thus while the following descriptions involve comparison to present designs, these analogies should be interpreted with caution. Designs are expected to evolve.

Appendix H

The U.S. Department of Energy and the Idaho National Laboratory are developing a program, the Next Generation Nuclear Plant (NGNP), for implementing the first Gen IV reactor designs, and have initiated discussions with potential private managers of the project.

Potential portions of this program are included in the above discussion of the GT-MHR and PBMR designs. The NGNP program anticipates completing the first Gen IV concept by 2020 and possibly earlier. Project efforts will include the production of hydrogen at the prototype reactor. While very high temperature gas-cooled reactors appear most likely for eventual consideration, additional U.S.-based Gen IV designs might be submitted to the program managers.

Nuclear Regulatory Commission officials have indicated that present staff at the NRC are not familiar with innovative reactor designs, thus any application for design certification would consume more time than for more evolutionary LWR designs. Because GIF reactors involve very long term plans, NRC familiarity with designs might evolve before Generation IV reactors are ready for design certification.

Gen IV programs are summarized on
http://www.inel.gov/initiatives/generation.shtml.

Gas-cooled Fast Reactor (GFR):

The GFR uses helium coolant directed to a gas turbine generator to produce electricity. This parallels PBMR and original GT-MHR designs. The primary difference from these designs is that the GFR would be a "fast" or breeder reactor. One favored aspect of the design is that it would minimize the production of many undesirable spent fuel waste streams. The reference design size was targeted to be 288 MWe with a deployment target date of 2025. In addition to producing electricity the design might be used as a process heat source in the production of hydrogen. For further information see http://nuclear.inl.gov/gen4/gfr.shtml

167

Appendix H

Lead-cooled Fast Reactor (LFR):

So far, most breeder reactors have used molten metal technologies for their coolants.

Many Fast Breeder Reactors (FBRs) have used molten sodium, a metal with which there is considerable experience but which has sometimes proven difficult to handle.

The LFR uses molten lead or a lead-bismuth alloy as its coolant.

Similar designs are being investigated in Russia which is not a GIF participant. Some designs favored under the Generation IV program would result in long periods between refueling, as much as 20 years or more. Target ranges for this reactor would be 50-150 MWe. That would be rather small by historic nuclear standards, but might meet localized market needs.

Designs as large as 1200 MWe have been suggested. Initial targeted deployment would be in 2025. Proposed designs would favor electricity production though proponents consider the production of process heat at LFRs as possible. For further information see http://nuclear.inl.gov/gen4/lfr.shtml.

One design in this family of reactors is described on http://www.coe.berkeley.edu/labnotes/1002/reactor.html

Molten Salt Reactor (MSR):

The MSR involves a circulating liquid of sodium, zirconium, and uranium fluorides as a reactor fuel though the design could use a wide variety of fuel cycles.

The MSR has been presented as providing a comparatively thorough fuel burn, safe operation, and proliferation resistance. The initial reference design would be 1000 MWe with a deployment target date of 2025. Temperatures would not be as hot as for some other advanced reactors, but some process heat potential exists. Versions of the MSR have been around for some time but were never commercially implemented. The MSR was down rated within the Gen IV program during 2003 because it was seen as too distant in the future for inclusion within the Gen IV schedule. At the same time proponents see some MSR potential for the NGNP program. For further information see http://nuclear.inl.gov/gen4/msr.shtml

Sodium-cooled Fast Reactor (SFR):

Sodium-cooled fast reactors have been the most popular design for breeder reactors.

Designs have been proposed under the Department of Energy's "roadmap" for Generation IV reactors ranging from 150 to 1700 MWe. Elements of the SFR are included in the 4S design proposed by Toshiba for Galena, Alaska. Molten metal technology is no longer "new" but several early SFR prototypes had difficulty obtaining sustained operation.

The BN-600 in Russia has been regarded as highly reliable. Design supporters believe that the SFR promises superior fuel management characteristics.

The original target deployment date of 2015 reflected the considerable research that the design has already received though the design is clearly not as ready for U.S. deployment as LWR designs being evaluated for roughly the same period. The target date seems to be lagging as the VHTR designs gain favor.

Prototypes have been built in France, Japan, Germany, the United Kingdom, Russia, India, and the United States starting as early as 1951. Initial deployment would probably focus on electricity due to comparatively low "outlet temperatures" for the design.

Appendix H

Supercritical-water-cooled Reactor (SCWR):

The SCWR design is to be the next step in LWR development and has been proposed with alternatives that evolve from both the BWR and the PWR. SCWRs would operate at higher temperatures and thermal efficiencies than present LWRs.

The reference plant might be 1700 MWe, at the upper end of present LWR designs. The deployment target date was 2025. Some GIF participants favor the SCWR design because it is more familiar to commercial markets than are more innovative concepts. Much of the design research has been in Japan. Designers intend the SCWR to be much less expensive to build than today's LWRs though some of these economies appear to be shared by units now undergoing certification or pre-certification. Operating cost savings are also anticipated.

For further information see http://nuclear.inl.gov/gen4/scwr.shtml

Very-high-temperature Reactor (VHTR):

The VHTR is an evolution from the HTGR family of reactors but would operate at even higher temperatures than designs now undergoing pre-certification. Some of the VHTR design standards might be met by modified PBMRs or GT-MHRs.

In contrast with the GFR, the VHTR would not be a breeder reactor, thus it would produce less potentially usable fuel than it consumes. In addition to generating electricity, the design can provide process heat for industrial activities including hydrogen production and desalinization. Deployment is targeted for 2020, earlier than most Generation IV designs. The VHTR is now a favored design in the U.S., where it is the basis for most anticipated submissions for the still-evolving Next Generation Nuclear Plant (NGNP). France also favors the design which is also popular in Asia and South Africa.

The VHTR is discussed at http://nuclear.inl.gov/gen4/vhtr.shtml and http://www.nuc.berkeley.edu/designs/mhtgr/mhtgr.html

Appendix I
Game Changing Technologies

Compact Fluorescent Lamps (CFL)

A 100 watt compact fluorescent lamps (CFL) uses 23 watts, or about 75% less power than a 100 watt incandescent bulb. The advantages of CFL's were discussed in Chapter 7.

Light Emitting Diodes (LED)[92]

LED lighting may be able to play an important role in conserving electricity as they are more energy efficient than Fluorescent or High Discharge lighting. Fluorescent and high intensity discharge (HID) lighting uses less electricity than incandescent lighting. Both fluorescent and HID lighting have been available for many years, and it is common to see fluorescent lighting in offices and in the low bays of factories and HID lighting in factory high bays.

Compact fluorescents were designed to replace incandescent lamps but their high first cost initially delayed acceptance by the public. This has now changed and the CFL can pay for itself in a few months. Fluorescent and high intensity discharge lamps require ballasts, a transformer like device that supplies the necessary high start up voltage and then regulates the current to maintain the arc in the lamp. These ballasts add cost which originally made compact fluorescent lamps several times more expensive than incandescent lamps.

Lighting is more complicated than it appears. Color, for example, can play an important role in the choice of the type of lamp to use. White light, or light that reasonably mimics sun light, renders the colors of items more accurately than fluorescent or some other types of lighting. This is why stores continue to use incandescent spot lighting to light their displays: Incandescent is accepted as white light which makes clothing and other items appear more attractive to shoppers.

Modern CFL's are said to do a better job of mimicking sunlight.

171

Appendix I

The amount of light on a surface is also an important factor when selecting lighting. Work surfaces such as desks and factory benches should have around 100 foot candles at their surfaces: Parking lots might have only 15 foot candles on their surfaces. There is a body of engineering work that describes the proper amount of light for various surfaces. Light diminishes as the square of its distance from the surface to the light source so the size or wattage and type of lamp has to be chosen with that factor in mind.

Light Emitting Diodes, LED's, are semi conducting devices that emit light when a current passes through them. The light has not been very bright but is emitted at a single wavelength making for pure colors and an ability to focus the light. Two benefits of LED's are their long life (100,000 hours versus 2000 hours for incandescent lamps) and low power requirements. LED's can be operated from batteries which has led to their quick adoption in the automotive arena for such applications as dome lights, license plate lighting and directional signals. LED's have also recently been used extensively in traffic lights.

New developments are increasing the light output (lumens per watt, where lumens are a measure of the amount of light) and the emitting of white light. LED's have the potential to replace incandescent bulbs and use approximately 90% less energy than an incandescent bulb.

Penetration of the market will depend largely on LED efficiency and price. In the same way that fluorescent lighting did not quickly replace incandescent lighting in residential applications, it is very possible that LED's will not achieve their full potential because of high first cost and how the user perceives color rendition and brightness.

LED's may help us make major strides in energy conservation.

LED's are an example of how new technologies can help conserve electricity.

172

Appendix I

Micro-turbines

Micro turbines produce between 25 and 500 kW of power. They are relatively less efficient than full size gas or steam turbines. They currently are more costly on a $ per installed kW basis.

They have been proposed as components of a distributed generating system, which is a highly controversial concept. The existing grid is built for safety and reliability. A distributed system could cause disruption to the grid. Studies are in progress to either prove or disprove this concern.

Micro turbines are being used at landfills to burn methane gas. They could conceivably be used in conjunction with anaerobic digesters on farms, hog farms or cattle feed lots to burn the methane gas produced from animal waste.

Micro turbines are still in the development stage.

NOTES

1 National Oceanic and Atmospheric Administration, March 31 2005 report
http://www.noaanews.noaa.gov/stories2005/s2412.htm

2 ANPR, Department of Commerce comments, page 59, and ANPR page
337

3 The Electric Power Research Institute (EPRI) April 27, 2007 and Pew
Climate Center

4 If it was too difficult to reduce CO_2 emissions, companies could pay $12
per metric ton of carbon. The fee would increase five percentage points
above the inflation rate every year.

5 EPRI April 27, 2007 and PEW Climate Center

6 There also are corresponding receipts to the government which raises a
separate issue: How will the government use this money? If the funds
aren't distributed to tax payers they will represent a hidden tax hike as the
cost of permits will be passed along to consumers. In addition the receipts
could be a piggy bank for Congress to use for their favorite projects.

7 Center on Budget and policy Priorities, *Designing Climate Change
Legislation that Shields Low Income Households from Increased Poverty
and Hardship*, May 9, 2008

8 NY Times, *Money and Lobbyists Hurt European Efforts to Curb Gases*,
December 10, 2008

9 John Vidal, *Eco Soundings*, The Guardian, October 22, 2008

10 Wall Street Journal, *Pollution Credits Let Dumps Double Dip*, October 20,
2008

11 Wall Street Journal February 9, 2007

12 As reported in the 2002 EIA report.

13 The 50% proposal is based on allowing CO_2 in the atmosphere to increase
slightly, while not allowing temperatures to rise more than 2 degrees C.
The UN's proposal to cut emissions world wide by 60% from 1990 levels
is to maintain CO_2 levels in the atmosphere at current levels. The UN
proposes that developed countries reduce emissions by 80% while
continuing to allow developing countries to increase emissions; overall
the world would achieve a 60% reduction.

175

NOTES

14 "The Intergovernmental Panel on Climate Change (IPCC) also showed that holding global warming to 2 degrees to 2.4 degrees Celsius would require an atmospheric concentration of 445 to 490 ppm of carbon dioxide equivalent. At the moment, the concentration of greenhouse gas emissions stands at around 430 ppm of carbon dioxide equivalent and, due to human activities, is increasing at a rate of nearly 3 ppm carbon dioxide equivalent per year. Under 'business as usual', they will reach 550 ppm of carbon dioxide equivalent by 2035. The IPCC data suggests it may be necessary to achieve a reduction in CO2 emissions approaching 100 per cent between 2000 and the year 2050, to stabilise atmospheric concentrations of greenhouse gases at a level of 450 ppm carbon dioxide equivalent or less." *Section 1.0.6 Zero Carbon Britain – Taking a Global Lead* by Liberal Democrats [UK] September 2007

15 Included in the United Nations Framework Convention on Climate Change (UNFCCC) or Rio Agreement, in the Kyoto Protocol and in The September 2007 Asia Pacific Economic Cooperation (APEC) Declaration.

16 From *Centre for International Sustainable Development Law (CISDL)* "A particularly important aspect of the principle is international assistance, including financial aid and technology transfer. As developed countries have played the greatest role in creating most global environmental problems, and have superior ability to address them, they are expected to take the lead on environmental problems. In addition to moving toward sustainable development on their own, developed countries are expected to provide financial, technological, and other assistance to help developing countries fulfill their sustainable development responsibilities. In *Agenda 21*, developed countries reaffirmed their previous commitments to reach the accepted UN target of contributing 0.7% of their annual gross national product to official development assistance" Extract from *"The Principle of Common But Differentiated Responsibilities: Origins and Scope For the World Summit on Sustainable Development,* 2002 Johannesburg, 26 August."

17 Study by Wolfgang Lutz, of the Austrian Academy of Science in Vienna, and Brian O'Neill, of the International Institute for Applied Systems Analysis in Laxenburg, Austria, 2003

18 Report of the Conference of the Parties on its thirteenth session held in Bali from 3 – 15 December, 2007, Addendum Part II

NOTES

19 EU Urged to Agree on Climate before UN Talks Open. Reuters, 1 October 2008

20 Fires may destroy Europe's emission trading scheme; Financial Times, August 2007.

21 Malta and Lithuania to join forces against EU CO2 caps; EurActiv Network, August 22, 2007

22 The Guardian, 3 April 2007

23 CLIMATE CHANGE LEGISLATION DESIGN WHITE PAPER, Scope of a Cap-and-Trade Program; *Prepared by the Committee on Energy and Commerce staff-October 2007*

24 The number of vehicles in the U.S. could increase from around 226 million in 2004 to around 321 million in 2050 due to population growth. By one calculation, if 80% of all vehicles on the road in 2050 had gasoline mileage of over 100 mpg, oil usage, and CO2 emissions, would be cut by approximately 50%. See *A Strategy for Achieving Independence from Foreign Oil*, at www.tsaugust.org

25 Financial Times, October 29, 2008

26 Communist philosophy: Each achieves according to his abilities and gets according to his needs.

27 Remarks by President elect Obama, November 18, 2008 at the Bi-Partisan Governors Climate Summit, arranged by California Governor Arnold Schwarzenegger.

28 David Derbyshire *New green law could ration flights and raise fuel prices*, The Daily Mail, 16 November 2007.

29 Power Magazine, November 19, 2008

30 California Energy Commission, *Proposed Standards For Residential and Nonresidential Buildings*, page 63, November 2007

31 US Energy Information Administration, Electric Power Monthly, March 2006, Tables 1.6b and 1.8b

32 See *The Future of Coal, Options for a Carbon Constrained World.* Massachusetts Institute of Technology (MIT) 2007: *and* Power Magazine, July 2007 for additional information on sequestration.

NOTES

33 *The Future of Coal, Options for a Carbon Constrained World,* MIT 2007

34 National Energy Technology Laboratory, *Carbon Sequestration Atlas of the United States and Canada*

35 EIA Table, *Net Generation by State by Sector, June 2008 and 2007*

36 See 49 CFR 195 for formula establishing pipeline parameters such as pipe thickness given pipeline pressure.

37 *Storage of Captured Carbon Dioxide Beneath Federal Lands,* U.S. Department of energy and *The International Petroleum Encyclopedia,* published by PennWell Corporation.

38 Text, *Pipeline Design and Construction,* by Mo Mohitpour et al.

39 Press release November 14, 2007 by the North American Carbon Capture & Storage Association (NACCSA),

40 Prairie State Energy facility, reported in Naperville and Geneva Illinois newspapers August and September 2007.

41 Malcolm Brinded, *Shared Trust –the Key to Secure LNG Supplies,* CEO Shell Gas & Power, 2003

42 American Petroleum Institute web site http://www.naturalgasfacts.org/factsheets/ocs.html 2008

43 Larger natural gas power plants, rated approximately 500 MW, have recently been built. These could be used as base load plants.

44 The Average size of wind turbines in 2006 was 1.6 MW with a total of 3,188 units installed in 2007. *Annual Report on U.S. Wind Power Installation, Cost, and Performance Trends:* Page 22, 2006

45 A more accurate way of defining capacity factor is to determine how much electricity in kWhrs is generated by a wind turbine over 24 hours during a 365 day period and then comparing this with the amount that could be generated at the rated name plate capacity over the same period.

46 *AWEA 2009 Market report,* January 2009. AWEA reported an increase in installed capacity of 8,358 MW. Assuming an average turbine size of 1.7 MW gives the number of installations. The total was helped by a large number of installations in December that may reduce the number of installations in 2009.

NOTES

47 *A Critical Evaluation of the Energy Plans and Actions Announced in April 2007 by New York's Governor, NYSERDA and New York PSC;* published by EMPA

48 Wall Street Journal, *Turbulence Ahead*, April 18, 2008

49 Industrial Wind Action Group, Wind Alert, October 16, 2008

50 *A Grand Plan for Solar Energy*, January 2008 issue of Scientific American.

51 Searchinger et al, *Use of U.S. Croplands for Biofuels Increases Greenhouse Gases Through Emissions from Land Use Change,* Science Magazine, February 2, 2008

52 Dennis Avery, *Biofuels, Food, or Wildlife? The Massive Land Costs of U.S. Ethanol.*

53 Ibid

54 From California CalCars

55 Article by Isidor Buchmann, *Cadex Electronics* - 4/18/2007

56 John Addison, *Lithium Battery Delays and Advancements* published in Clean Fleet Report, 8/13/07.

57 The Volt is slightly different than other proposed PHEV's. The Volt will use a small gasoline engine for recharging the battery while deriving its power for operating the car from its battery; not from the small gasoline engine. PHEV's, similar to the prototypes, will use the gasoline engine to power the car at speeds over around 40 mph and rely on the battery for powering the car at slower speeds. These batteries will be recharged from a standard 120 volt outlet.

58 See *A Strategy for Achieving Independence from Foreign Oil*, www.tsaugust.org

59 Department of Energy, *Annual Energy Outlook 2009*, March 2009

60 Michael Kintner-Meyer, Kevin Schneider, Robert Pratt, *Impacts Assessment of Plug-in Hybrid Vehicles on Electric Utilities and Regional US Power Grids,* Pacific Northwest National Laboratory.

179

NOTES

61 The Pacific Northwest National Laboratory report Table 2, shows a total of 91 million vehicles being recharged during the 12 hour overnight off peak period. This is 30% of the 321 million vehicles forecast to be on the road in 2050.

62 U.S. Department of Energy. Also Environmental Protection Agency, *Clean Alternative Fuels: Compressed Natural Gas* pdf

63 *Hydrogen Today, April 2004*; published by TSAugust, a Think tank based in Reston Virginia.

64 Source: Energy Information Administration (EIA), Department of Energy.

65 According to the EIA approximately 89 percent of commercial building floor space already use fluorescent or High Intensity Discharge (HID) lighting.

66 An LED, or light-emitting diode, is essentially a semiconductor chip that emits light when it comes in contact with electricity.

67 A CFL rated 100 watts costing $2.00 compared with the $0.60 cost of an incandescent bulb, will save its higher incremental cost when burned four hours per day for 45 days.

68 Environmental Law Policy Center

69 Wall Street Journal 8/23/07

70 High density and mixed use construction around metro-stations have been touted as a way to reduce automobile usage. The presumption is that people will use mass transit and bicycles and have no need for cars. Some people will meet this profile, but there are strong arguments that people will still own automobiles and prefer to live in single family homes rather than mixed use areas. No one is predicting that millions of Americans will adopt these living environments.

71 City savings estimates of annual savings in Washington DC of $505 and annual savings in Chicago Illinois of $300, taken from U.S. Department of Energy, *energystar.gov/ windows_ methodology*, pdf 2006.

72 Calculation based on double hung Anderson series 200 windows, for a 2,000 square foot building. (Continued pg 181)

NOTES

The average volume usage of natural gas of 888 therms was from Energy Information Administration, *Residential Natural Gas Prices: What Consumers Should Know 1997,*

The number of households = 101.5 million; the. percentage of single family homes = 73%; and the percentage heating with natural gas = 53%, taken from. Energy Information Administration, *Residential Energy Overview 1997 for the United States*

73 Power Magazine, *Appellate court upholds Indiana commission's approval of IGCC plant,* October 21, 2008

74 "German chancellor Angela Merkel and others [are] suggesting that a per-capita emissions quota be considered when it comes to fair burden sharing in the future." From *Deutsche Welle,* 10 September 2007.

75 GDP per capita based on purchasing power. From the *International Monetary Fund.*

76 Honorable Vaclav Klaus, presentation, 2008 International Conference on Climate Change, New York

77 Federal Highway Administration and *Vehicle Ownership* by the European Environment Agency

78 Liberal Democrats [UK] , *Zero Carbon Britain – Taking a Global Lead,* September 2007

79 Ibid

80 Fredrik Bergstrom and Robert Gidehag, *EU vs US,* June 2004

81 Ibid

82 *Trends in Residential Air-Conditioning Usage from 1978 to 1997,* from DOE EIA

83 Liberal Democrats [UK], *Zero Carbon Britain – Taking a Global Lead,* September 2007

84 Clayton M. Christensen, *The Innovators Dilemma, When New Technologies Cause Great Firms to Fail,* Harvard Busines School Press

85 Edwin Lyman, Senior Scientist, Union of Concerned Scientists, Washington, DC *Letter to Editor,* Wall Street Journal, June 30, 2009

NOTES

86 (Appendix B) Extracted from TSAugust report, *False Promise of Renewable Energy*. Refer to original document for supporting notes.

87 (Appendix D) Ibid

88 (Appendix D) *A Grand Plan for Solar Energy*, January 2008 issue of Scientific American.

89 Appendix E) Battery recharging data from Pacific Northwest National Laboratory report

90 (Appendix E) Data on the number of vehicles from *A Strategy for Achieving Independence from Foreign Oil*, TSAugust. Vehicles refers to cars and light trucks SUV's)

91 Appendix H prepared by Neil Midkiff

92 Appendix I. Portions extracted from *America's Challenge* published by TSAugust in March, 2004

INDEX

INDEX

INDEX

INDEX

ABOUT THE AUTHOR

Donn Dears is a retired General Electric Company executive with extensive experience in power generation, transmission, distribution and related equipment.

He has been involved with servicing heavy equipment worldwide, while working with the oil, electric utility, steel, mining and transportation industries.

He was instrumental in establishing businesses for GE in the Middle East, Australia and Europe to serve the oil and natural gas industries.

He is currently president of TSAugust, a Think Tank comprised of volunteers concerned about energy and environmental issues.

TSAugust is a not for profit 501 (C) 3 corporation.

Dears graduated with honors from the United States Merchant Marine Academy with a B.S. degree in engineering and served on active duty in the U.S. Navy during the Korean War.

He is a graduate of GE's Manufacturing Management Program and of GE's prestigious General Management School at Crotonville, NY.